Contents

I Like Church, But...

J. Daniel Lupton

Destiny Image® Publishers, Inc.
P.O. Box 310
Shippensburg, PA 17257-0310

"Speaking to the Purposes of God
for This Generation
and for the Generations to Come"

ISBN 1-56043-183-0

For Worldwide Distribution
Printed in the U.S.A.

Fourth Printing: 1997 Fifth Printing: 1997

This book and all other Destiny Image
and Treasure House books are
available at Christian bookstores
and distributors worldwide.

For a U.S. bookstore nearest you,
call **1-800-722-6774**.
For more information on foreign distributors,
call **717-532-3040**.
Or reach us on the Internet:
http://www.reapernet.com

Introduction

I could have given up on church a long time ago. Some of my friends already have. They still claim to be Christians; it's just that they don't attend church anymore.

Don't they understand that Jesus loves His church? Aren't they aware that the church represents His body in the world? I guess these truths take a backseat to the hurts people have received in church settings of one kind or another.

Just about anybody who's been in church for very long has his or her own painful story to tell about gossip, hypocrisy, or racial snubs from fellow believers. Too many well-intentioned members of the body of Christ have felt unappreciated, have been forced into a mold they didn't fit, or chafed when told they couldn't do something because they were women or were too young or were old-fashioned.

Maybe purple ink should have been used in this Introduction just to remind us of the spiritual bruises and welts suffered by church people. Pastors know what I'm referring to. So do parishioners!

If someone gave you a bumper sticker that read, "I like church," would you display it on your car? All of us have had many good experiences that underscore such feelings. But is it a completely honest expression? I suspect most Christians would have some reservations. To tell it like it is, they would need a bumper sticker that reads, "I like church, but...."

There must be a thousand ways to finish that sentence. *I like church, but....* Even so, I suspect that rather than risk exposing their hurts, the majority of people actively involved in the life of a congregation would smile and say, "That's enough. Just leave it like it is, with the three little fill-in-the-blank dots there."

Dan Lupton has written the kind of book that uncovers some of the pain people experience in the body. Yet he's positive about the church, not negative. I don't believe he could write negatively about the church if he tried. His love for local congregations is obvious. Still, he's not ignorant of the fact that far too many people have been wounded in the house of the Lord.

What I like is how he holds up the ideal. He enables us to envision what the church being the church really looks like. Then he seeks to create in us an intense longing for that dream to become a reality.

What would our churches be like if some of the more embarrassing flaws were eliminated? Getting our minds around these issues can be extremely helpful. Doing so allows us to evaluate whether or not it's worth it to continue believing that the best can still be experienced.

No, I haven't given up on the church yet. I share a deep-seated desire to be part of what Dan writes about. Reading his words gives hope and encourages me to play my part in helping pull off what could be. It puts past pains into a proper perspective. I believe this book will do the same for you. If thousands of other readers have a similar response, Dan Lupton has done a great service for the church he loves so deeply.

David Mains

1

I Like Church, But
I Wish It Worked at Being
a Caring Family

Whoever does God's will
is My brother and sister and mother.
—*Jesus*, Mark 3:35

"Oh, she's the cutest of them all." A PanAm flight attendant responded that way when I asked if she had seen our baby. Although she might have given the same praise to each of the 12 children on the overseas flight, she recognized the name of ours. We had been childless through several years of marriage, and now Nancy and I were adopting a little Korean girl. The Lord answered our longing to be parents and also supplied a four-month-old orphaned baby with a family. "God sets the lonely in families," the psalmist wrote (Ps. 68:6a), and the three of us proved it. The thrill of that day is forever beautifully etched in our memories.

But we have other memories of that year. Nancy and I were learning that loneliness wears different faces, and God has many ways to set the lonely in families. We were pioneering a church planting in the intermountain Rockies when we adopted Amy. Our church opened in a five-dollar-a-Sunday rented American Legion Hall. Arriving early each Lord's Day, we started our setup routine by clearing tables of poker chips and shot glasses so we could teach Bible classes. In this unlikely setting, God soon entrusted us with many spiritual children who needed a family.

There was the poor family from Texas, lonely in this mountain environment, and the helicopter pilot who found himself employed far from his eastern roots. One family had followed the interstate road construction work to our town, just like people followed the laying of the railroad tracks years ago. The money was good, but they were lonely in Utah. Two Christian college students from Taiwan struggled with typical young adult loneliness, in addition to the separation from their homeland. A prosperous manufacturer's family also became a part of this fellowship. They were driven to us by spiritual hunger and—you guessed it—loneliness. Yet the lonely didn't all come from outside the state. Many others who loved Jesus felt alone, even though they had lived their entire lives in that Utah town.

As the Lord had placed Amy in our family, so He placed these people in another family of His making—the church. Sundays weren't only worship times; they were family gatherings. Church picnics and dinners were our family reunions.

The lonely can be found not only in Utah towns, but also in coastal megacities, Alaska fly-in villages, Florida retirement communities, Toronto suburbs, and wherever people live and wish to live a little more. I know God doesn't always give parents to the orphan or a spouse to the single person. But I believe He chooses to set many lonely people in families by placing them in caring churches.

A Longing for Family Relationships

After I spoke in their church, Lee and Dorothy took me to their home for a hospitable break between services. We talked about the warm atmosphere that prevailed in their congregation. "I've become quite a hugger in recent years," Dorothy offered. She also confided that her parents didn't hug her when she was young.

"My parents weren't huggers either," I replied, "but I never doubted that they loved me." Dorothy, a beautiful retired lady in her sixties, told me she didn't know that her mother had ever loved her. The conversation turned quiet and wistful. Her mom had been attractive and liked to be fussed over. The children, however, were made to feel like they were a nuisance.

Forty years after leaving home, Dorothy still longed to be loved. Healing in this life would be partial for her—a foretaste of the full healing of Heaven. Through the years Dorothy's needs had been met through the devotion of Lee and their children, the love of Jesus, and the care given and received in this special church, which had been central to their lives. They raised their children there, rejoiced in spiritual victories and seasons of renewal the Lord had granted, and wept with friends in life's tragedies. As they reminisced about the past four decades, I didn't hear one mention of a church program. But Dorothy and Lee spoke freely of pastors they admired, friends they loved, and people they missed who had died or moved away. Life had been good for them, and it continues to be so because of their caring church family.

Thousands of churches are like that. Unfortunately, stories like Freida's are also prevalent. Freida and I had worked together, but we never worshiped together. She was a lovely and sensitive lady who went through a lonely, painful time of marital crisis. When I called to check up on her, Freida thanked me for my interest. She also volunteered the information that no one from her church had called or shown concern for how she was doing. As I talked to her I thought of a bumper sticker by a Chicago Cubs enthusiast: "I Love [*heart*] the Cubs," and then in smaller letters, "But I Long for a Pennant." (Cub fans, who haven't been to the World Series since Nero was Emperor, certainly understand.) My friend Freida was thinking, "I like church, but I wish it worked at being a caring family." Others in churches all around the world have their own "I Like Church, But..." bumper-sticker wishes.

The word *church* is benign to a few, but emotionally charged to many. The emotions usually relate to healthy or unhealthy church family experiences. David Mains's "You Need to Know" Christian television program has interviewed dozens of guests who have shared a one-minute Warm Church Memory. These 60-second spots are often from Christian leaders in their fifth or sixth decade who joyfully recount memories from childhood church days. The word *church* brings happy recollections of classes and clubs, musicals and pageants, picnics and potlucks, but especially people. Most Warm Church Memories focus on a teacher or preacher or friend who made faith easier and life more valuable through how he or she lived and loved. In many traditions these friends were considered family and were called "Brother" or "Sister."

By *emotionally charged* I also recognize that some people have experienced hurts and disappointments that stimulate flinching or cringing at the mention of "church." Their expectations have been marred through quarrels and divisions, criticism and control, neglect and betrayal.

I long for churches to consistently get it right when it comes to being caring families. I wish all church experiences were like Dorothy's and none were like Freida's. I yearn for church memories to always be warm. The more our culture is marked by dysfunctional family traits, the more important it is for churches to function as families of faith and love. How can we do this? We must follow the cues of Jesus and the apostles.

Calvary Gave New Meaning to *Family*

God has always had a family plan. Adam and Eve were created a family. God promised Abraham that through his family all the people of the earth would be blessed (see Gen. 12:3). Jesus Himself was born into a family, enjoying a father, mother, brothers, and sisters (see Mt. 13:55-56).

But early in His life, there were clues that Jesus would give new meaning to *family*. One clue came when, at age 12, Jesus alarmed His parents with a disappearing act. Joseph and Mary lost their son at the great Feast of the Passover. To their relief they found Him in the temple courts talking to the teachers. Mary asked, "Son, why have You treated us like this? Your father and I have been anxiously searching for You." Jesus' answer was as puzzling as His conduct. "Why were you searching for Me?...Didn't you know I had to be in My Father's house?" (Lk. 2:48-49).

Another clue came while Jesus taught a standing-room-only crowd. His earthly family arrived, but there wasn't room for them. Someone whispered to Jesus that His mother and brothers were outside and wanted to see Him. " 'Who are My mother and My brothers?' He asked. Then He looked at those seated in a circle around Him and said, 'Here are My mother and My brothers! Whoever does God's will is My brother and sister and mother' " (Mk. 3:33-35).

But it was on the cross itself that *family* was confirmed as more than nuclear. Jesus had brothers, but they did not yet believe in Him as they later would. Mary was a widow by this time, and the brothers had left her to endure her Son's death alone. They could not be depended on for continued support. "When Jesus saw His mother there, and the disciple whom He loved standing nearby, He said to His mother, 'Dear woman, here is your son,' and to the disciple, 'Here is your mother.' From that time on, this disciple took her into his home" (Jn. 19:26-27). Faith and love, rather than genes and chromosomes, would define *family* for Christ's followers.

From the beginning, churches were cast in the role of caring families. People in the early church had to care for one another because of the immense persecution suffered under a Jewish leader named Saul of Tarsus. Then one day Jesus, in His resurrected glory, appeared to Saul. Blinded by the experience,

Saul spent three days repenting, praying, and waiting for the teacher whom Jesus said would come and heal him. Imagine the emotion of the moment when Ananias finally arrived. Just picture him giving this enemy of the church a hug, saying, "Brother Saul, the Lord—Jesus, who appeared to you on the road as you were coming here—has sent me so that you may see again..." (Acts 9:17). With the name "Brother," Ananias welcomed this recent anti-Christian terrorist into the family of God. A few days earlier Saul viewed the Damascus church as a religious sect to be hated and destroyed. Now he found it was his new family.

Saul became Paul the evangelist and apostle. Scholars today refer to his work as church planting, but Paul might have preferred to call it family planning. He didn't organize church members; he gave birth to spiritual children and introduced believers in Christ to their new brothers and sisters. Instead of parliamentary procedure, Paul and the other apostles taught Christians how to love and protect their fellow family members: "Love the brotherhood of believers" (1 Pet. 2:17b). "If your brother is distressed because of what you eat, you are no longer acting in love" (Rom. 14:15a). "I commend to you our sister Phoebe" (Rom. 16:1a). "Brothers, do not slander one another" (Jas. 4:11a).

Just as families are not perfect, so churches are not perfect. They weren't in the beginning, and they haven't been in any era of history. But churches are families, and good families give mutual care. I sense there is a renewed hunger for this aspect of church life. Researcher George Barna confirms, "Church-goers agree that they are taking home strong doses of 'head knowledge' every week; but relatively few claim that they are warmed by the feeling of belonging to a loving and caring body."[1]

Calvary reveals the church family as Christ intended it—caring for the grieving widows and welcoming the worst of sinners when they come to faith in Him. Wouldn't it be wonderful to experience a church family that really works that way?

Caring Establishes Value

If we could put a stethoscope to the hearts of those we know, our listening ears would detect unsoundness in people's perception of their value. Company downsizing, marriage failures, recreational sex, child abuse, drive-by shootings, and movie mayhem all cause many to doubt they are of inestimable worth. The church, on the other hand, has the privilege and responsibility to appreciate and enhance everyone's value.

Ron is a teacher who became president of a Christian college. As a young man raised by

---

1.   George Barna, *Vital Signs* (Westchester, IL: Crossway Books, 1984), 132.

a single mom, Ron received no positive impressions from the church until he reached the fifth grade. That year his Sunday school teacher called him on a Friday evening: "Ron, I'm going fishing tomorrow and I've got an extra rod. If fishing interests you, I'd love to have you come along." Ron felt like a real person, important enough to be chosen over all the adult men his teacher might have invited.

On the lake, Ron's new hero lit a cigarette while patiently instructing him in the basics of fishing. After a few fish had been netted, the teacher gave Ron his life testimony. Ron learned how important Jesus was to his teacher. The God-led man was really fishing for a boy that morning, for that was the day Ron accepted Jesus as Savior and began his lifetime adventure with the Lord.

When Ron tells the story, he smilingly mentions that if the executive board had known that the teacher smoked, they would have disqualified him from having a class. But this man was the only person in the church who cared enough to invest time in Ron and speak to him about his relationship with Jesus Christ. Through this experience, Ron's life was upgraded in his own estimation from "not worth much to anyone" to "a person of great value with a purpose and a future."

Churches can give value to people the same way healthy families do. Families celebrate the victories and accomplishments of family members. The Hebrew nation had celebrations that lasted more than a week. For instance, the Feast of Tabernacles was a thanksgiving praise festival with a family atmosphere. This feast provided family involvement for servant workers, and even "the aliens, the fatherless and the widows who live in your towns" were invited (Deut.16:14). God's program has always been set in the context of families who care. For those lacking nuclear family care, God provides a family of faith and love in the church.

Our faith may be the very reason we need a church family. Having preached in the open air to several hundred people in rural India, I gave an invitation to turn from idols to the one true God and His Son, the Savior Jesus Christ. As many responded publicly to become Christians, my interpreter whispered in my ear, "That lady in the blue and that teenager on the right will not be able to go home. Their conversion to Christ means they will never be welcomed back. We'll take them into our homes tonight and find new living arrangements for them in the next few days." The church literally became their family.

In North America, second- and third-generation Christians often can't appreciate the breadth and intensity of family emotions when someone puts his or her trust in Christ. Others know the pain all too well. When my wife, Nancy, was awakened to faith as a high school sophomore, her father was furious.

She wasn't kicked out of home—the door locks weren't re-keyed. But her need for a family of faith to affirm and value her was agonizingly obvious.

Families value their members with celebration in times of rejoicing and comfort in times of weeping. "Share with God's people who are in need…. Rejoice with those who rejoice; mourn with those who mourn" (Rom. 12:13,15). My father went home to the Lord 14 years ago and my mother 6 years ago. The love of the church family I grew up in and the love of the church I was pastoring are what I remember most from those two funerals. Hugs, prayers, food, and warm memories were shared for days. The church was my family. It gave value to both the living and the departed.

The greedy, lustful human race has been devalued by its own warring deeds. Yet the birth, life, and death of the Son of God puts great worth on even the most supposedly worthless person. Jesus loves us, cares for us, and wants to be one with us. He valued us by going to Calvary to redeem every soul. He gives each of us the opportunity to affirm that value by treating those whom He loves as He would treat them.

How Does a Family Show It Cares?

When we look at the life of Jesus and reflect on our own experiences, we can discern common characteristics in caring families and churches.

A Family Cares in the Big Moments.

Births, weddings, illnesses, and graduations are some of the bigger events in our lives. At these times we want a family who cares. My granddaughter, Gini, is in kindergarten. Last week I enjoyed hearing her sing a Christmas song. It caught my ear because it was several months past Christmas. "Gini, where did you learn that song?" I asked.

"That's from my school Christmas program," Gini told me, "the program you didn't come to." *Oops.* I heard a tinge of sadness in her voice. A grandpa ought to be there for big events like kindergarten Christmas programs. What stuck in her memory was not that her performance was early in December while I was out of town conducting conferences for church leaders. Five months after the event she only remembered that I hadn't been there.

Jesus was there for the big events in His family. His first miracle was the changing of water to wine at a wedding. We don't know the names of the two who exchanged their covenant vows, but Jesus was in attendance with His mother, who was obviously more than a guest—she felt responsible for wedding refreshments. These people were probably family to Mary and Jesus.

In junior high school I had pneumonia and was admitted to Mercy Hospital. My parents and my Aunt Betty came to visit. My pastor came to see me, and my Sunday school class wrapped a few silly gifts for me to open one day at a time. Pneumonia was a big thing in my life, and my church came through with family-style care. That's the way churches need to be!

A Family Also Cares in the Little Courtesies.

It's the little kindnesses that change a model house into a model home. *Please* and *thank you* still work wonders. "I'll take out the garbage" works too. It's a mystery why some couples are more courteous to strangers than to each other. The family has to be upheld by little touches of everyday blessings.

A courtesy can be as simple as a compliment. At the end of a day, when you reflect on the brighter moments, they are likely to include any words of praise. When someone you respect says, "You did outstanding work on this project," you smile. Hours later you still feel the glow of that applause.

At church we have the power to lift someone with the right words. When Jesus met Nathanael, He looked him in the eye and said, "Here is a true Israelite, in whom there is nothing false" (Jn. 1:47b). Nathanael had been a whiny, disillusioned person who had given up on religion. He was best known for the easy criticism that came to his tongue. If Jesus had wanted to play Don Rickles and make some cutting remark, He had a wealth of material to use. There was one good thing, however, about Nathanael. He was honest, even in his disillusionment. Jesus ignored

Nathanael's less admirable qualities and complimented him on his one good feature. Nathanael forgot his cynicism and 30 seconds later declared, "Rabbi, You are the Son of God; You are the King of Israel" (Jn. 1:49b).

A simple caring conversation like that can turn a life to the good forever. We need to look for the opportunities at church to build up someone, add value, and encourage. Caring can mean a card in the mail, a breakfast together, or a phone call. When someone shares a prayer need, huddle with that person immediately and pray. A little caring courtesy can be as simple as sharing a soft drink, or even a cup of water.

Family-Style Care Values People Over Image.

One of the frequent barriers to caring for others is an exaggerated importance placed on image. I've known Christian educators to treat pupils unfairly, even harshly, because of their concern about what a school visitor might observe. Some churchgoers are more passionate about church property than people. A coworker once told me that since his church had installed new carpeting, they limited weekday youth clubs to families of church members. It would mar their image to have a carpet smudge or a mark on a wall. A teenager left his church of five years after receiving criticism for the brass solo he played in an evening service. His style didn't fit their image.

If image had been an issue with Jesus, He would not have traveled around with fishermen, visited with a Samaritan woman, or dined with Zacchaeus. The public response was, "He has gone to be the guest of a 'sinner' " (Lk. 19:7b). But you'll look in vain for an occasion when Jesus refrained from caring for someone because of how it might hurt His image.

Family Care Happens in Small Groups.

I know two large extended families who rent community centers for Christmas and Thanksgiving gatherings. With 120 to 200 relatives, they've outgrown the capacity to meet in a home. It has become impossible for a person to remember the details of each second-cousin-twice-removed! But they all love each other. How? Each person relates more intimately to a smaller family unit, and through the strong links of the family chain, they are bonded to the whole clan.

Your church is like an extended family of faith. You need to relate to the whole church "clan" in worship and joy. But you may be able to best do that by first relating to a smaller group in which people know you better, miss you when you can't be there, and give extra attention in times of unusual need. What are these smaller groups called? No uniform nomenclature has been established; small groups can be all kinds of things. For 200 years these smaller units were often Sunday school classes. Today they are called covenant groups, elder care groups, cell groups, youth groups, discipleship groups, support groups, ministry teams, fellowships, Timothy groups...the list goes on. If I'd kept the bulletins from all the churches I've visited in the last three years, I could fill up a page with titles for these small groups. The names may be new, but the concept is as old as church history. Two hundred fifty years ago John Wesley, founder of Methodism, had support groups called "bands," "select societies," and "classes."[2] Can you name the small groups in your church? If you want to be a cared-for family member, enter into one.

Family-Style Care Requires Time.

Caring means commitment, and for many people, time is more important than money. Even the simplest acts of caring require time. A conversation that would bless a friend's life may go unspoken because of the rush from church to home for a football game. My parents had time margins that allowed for spontaneously inviting company over after church or for assisting someone in need right away. When we plan our church comings and goings to match the scheduled service times or the *TV Guide*, we eliminate the margin to care for one another. Jesus tells the story of the robbed and beaten man who was ignored

---

2. Ingvar Haddal, *John Wesley* (New York: Abingdon Press, 1961), 102.

by two passersby before a Samaritan took
time to come to his aid (see Lk. 10:30-35). It
may be that those who passed him didn't feel
any sympathetic nudgings to help—or it may
be they wanted to care, but their next appointment was too pressing to allow them to
stop. Don't let that become your excuse. If
you want to be cared for, you must take the
time to care for others.

Family Care Begins With Listening.
Jesus was a great listener. His caring
deeds came from His listening habits. When
Jesus went to the wedding in Cana of Gali-
lee, He didn't barge in, take over, and give or-
ders. He mingled and waited. When His
mother told Him about the problem of running out of wine, Jesus listened. Only after
He fully heard the need did He ask that the
water pots be filled. The miracle began with
listening.

For some of us the miracle *is* listening.
The better half of communication is listening. We should always be listening, even before we try to help someone. Listening may
be all the caring needed. One wise person
suggested that we take a tip from nature:
Our ears aren't made to shut, but our mouths
are.

Meeting the Family
I remember the first time Nancy met my
family. I was tense because I wanted my family to make a good impression. I would have

been more nervous if I'd realized that in meeting my family Nancy was seeing another picture of me. She may not have known it at the time, but she really married my family. I'm increasingly conscious of how my thoughts are like my dad's or my mother's. I even look like my dad looked when Nancy first met him. (It's a good thing she ignored the warning and married me anyway!)

In the same manner, a personal relationship with God comes through a family context. When we think about it, none of us would know about Jesus if we hadn't been told about Him and shown what He looks like by members of His family. So when someone wants to know about Jesus, the best place to inquire is where His family meets—at church.

One Sunday I met a beautiful young lady who was visiting church for the third time. A few weeks earlier, while sitting in a car dealership confused about whether to buy a new car or fix her old one, Nina called desperately to God. The impression immediately came to fix the car. An anticipated $600 repair expense melted down to a 99-cent spark plug. She was so thrilled with this answer to prayer that a hunger for God was stirred in her. What she did next was typical. Nina looked for a church nearby and visited. At this church, before she met Christ, Nina met His family.

She enjoyed the singing and the message at her first visits. She also listened to how people talked to each other. She heard an open invitation to a fiftieth wedding anniversary. She saw hugs exchanged and felt the pride of a handicapped boy being affirmed for learning to read and being complimented on his new suit. Nina told her auto story in the church narthex that third Sunday as a circle of newfound brothers and sisters gathered around to listen and rejoice in God's answer to her prayers. Her face shone with joy in the telling and receiving of her spark-plug experience. Though she was new to the church, she felt like it was a family reunion.

It was. Every Sunday is a family reunion. Nina found God through His family, a family who cared. It all began at Calvary where Jesus committed His grief-stricken mother to a leader in His new church. Christ continues to set the lonely in families. When He wonders where to place His children, He looks for churches that stimulate Warm Church Memories, not "I Like Church, But..." bumper sticker-type comments. Jesus longs for a church that is always eager to welcome and care for one more family member. I'm that way too. What about you?

> A person can pretend to care,
> but a person can't pretend to be there.

❖ ❖ ❖

If e'er to bless thy sons
My voice or hands deny,
These hands let useful skill forsake,
This voice in silence die.
                    —*Timothy Dwight*

❖ ❖ ❖

Kindness has influenced more people
than eloquence.

Make It Happen

*These suggestions will help you become a
more caring church family member.*

Individuals

1. *Work on your listening skills.* One way
to show you care is by remembering what
you've heard. So when a brother or sister
from your church expresses a special need,
don't forget to follow up on it. Imagine how
loved you'd feel if someone said, "I remember
you said you were working too hard. Have
things eased up for you?" or, "You mentioned
your daughter had a cold. Is she feeling better?" If you have trouble remembering things,
the old tie-a-string-around-your-finger trick
has proved a great reminder! Better yet, write
the need on a piece of paper and tuck it inside
your Bible or prayer journal so you'll be sure
to pray for your church family.

2. *Practice asking good questions.* Sometimes it's hard for people to open up enough
to share their thoughts and feelings. A caring person will gently probe others to find
out what's really going on inside. When you
talk to someone, go beyond surface questions
that define a person by his or her occupation,
place of residence, or relationships. Ask
what's-really-important-to-*you* questions,
like "When you have a free afternoon, how do
you like to spend it?" or "What's the one thing
about parenting that you've enjoyed the
most?" Mentally note the questions that

bring the most rewarding responses so that you can use them again. For a more in-depth discussion of this topic and for many creative ideas, consider reading the book *Getting Beyond "How Are You?"* by David Mains and Melissa Mains Timberlake. Call 1-800-2CHAPEL to order.

3. *Pray on the spot.* An uplifting way to end a conversation is by taking the problems you've discussed to the Lord. You don't need to make this a big production; simply say, "Can I pray for you about that right now?" Then, put your arm around your friend, or bow your head with him or her, and restate the concern in a sentence or two to the Lord. Conclude your prayer by asking for God's presence and by thanking Him for your friend and His love for you both. You can also end a telephone conversation by asking, "Can I pray for you before we hang up?" Thank God for being a part of your conversation and for being the One who is concerned about the needs of His family.

Families

4. *Set up a stationery shop.* Collect cards or nice note paper to send to people who are sick or hurting. On the way home from church, review any needs family members heard expressed. At home, play "post office" for an hour in the afternoon, sending a kindly get-well card to a friend from Bible Class, a thinking-of-you note to a shut-in, or a sympathy card to someone who has lost a family

member. During the week, be sure to re-stock the "shop" with stamps and handmade or sale-bought cards, note paper, and stickers. When it comes to creating your stationery shop, don't forget to use resources from computers, schools, and public libraries, as well as Christian bookstores.

5. *Chart your caring.* Post a "shepherd's chart" on your pantry door or refrigerator so you can keep track of your kids' caring acts. Begin by drawing or pasting on a cut-out of a shepherd. Then, each time your children tell you about an opportunity Jesus has given them to show care to one of His family members, or "sheep," let them add a sticker of a lamb (or color in one of the dozen sheep you have drawn). Plan a special outing for your little caretakers to celebrate when the whole shepherd's chart is full of cared-for sheep.

6. *Play the "What's Good About" Game.* Frequent affirmation of each other's strengths is one of the healthy characteristics of a caring family. When children feel good about themselves, they are better able to care for others. Once each day, spend time telling each other "What's good about" every family member. Sit in a circle (around a meal, perhaps) and take turns finishing the sentence "One thing I really like about (fill in a circle-member's name) is..." Affirmation becomes natural with practice. You'll find it will soon "spill over" into your church family as well.

Churches

7. *Start a Prayer & Care Network.* Like a prayer chain, this is a quick and efficient way to pass along special concerns. When something comes up, the prayer requestor calls the network head. He or she calls two people, who call two others, who call two others, until the whole congregation knows what's happening. Those at the "top" of the chain can not only express the prayer request, but also locate volunteers to meet any urgent emotional or physical needs. For example, while sharing the sad news about an upcoming funeral, ask for people to take meals to the family of the deceased person during the week. When a young dad is facing emergency surgery, find out who can help care for the children while his wife is with him in the hospital. When someone is sick, look for a card sender or a "tea and chicken soup" visitor. Make sure volunteer need meeters call the Prayer & Care Network head so things stay organized and work is not overlapped. Prayers are a great support for difficult times, and meeting an immediate need is a sure sign of God's family care.

8. *Keep track of the "regulars."* Take an inventory of ongoing needs: hospitalizations, new baby arrivals, the elderly and home-bound, missionaries, and so on. Then suggest ways congregation members can help to meet those—by setting up a "floating hospital chaplaincy," or a "home-cooked-meal team,"

furnishing and maintaining an open guest room on the church's second floor, starting a once-a-month work day, or whatever. Post this list in your foyer or fellowship hall where everyone can see it, and let people sign up for the team they'd like to join or the responsibility they can take. Then, use the sign-up as a calling list to gather caring people whenever the church family members are in need.

9. *Hold a family dinner.* Church potlucks are practically a Christian institution; why not use them to intentionally build family relationships? Supply the following questions for conversation during an after-church potluck. You may want to place a notebook at each table so someone can record what "family members" say. After dinner, have the folks sitting at each table pray together for the expressed needs. Lead a concluding prayer with the whole church family.

- What good things are happening in your life? Has anything occurred lately that requires special strength and encouragement from your church family?

- If you could send out an SOS message right now, what would it say?

- What's your idea of a perfect family? Of course you won't experience absolute perfection here on earth, but is there some way we can fill in where your immediate family or a previous church left off?

2

I Like Church, But I Wish It Would Capture the Heart of the Community

Neither do people light a lamp and
put it under a bowl. Instead they put
it on its stand, and it gives light to
everyone in the house.
—*Jesus*, Matthew 5:15

"What's that building look like inside?"
Pastor Bob asked his father as they waited in
their car for a stoplight to change.

"A lodge group of some kind meets there,"
was the older man's response, "but I've never
been inside, so I have no idea what it looks
like."

"What happens when they meet? What do
they do in there?"

Bob's dad said he really didn't know.

"Aren't you interested, or even a little
curious?"

"No, not really—never gave it a thought 'til now."

"Maybe that's the story of our church," Pastor Bob reflected as they drove on. "We have a nice building and it's on a major highway. I'm sure thousands in the community drive by our sanctuary daily. But they've never stopped at our church, much less come inside. It's like there's an invisible wall between us. They don't know what we do, and they probably don't even care."

Who wants to be part of something that most passersby aren't interested in or even a little curious about? Who wants to invest major resources in a cause others seldom give a thought to? Who wants to look back 25 years from now and say, "Our efforts really didn't amount to all that much, did they?" Who wants to face God knowing you represented His Son in a way that made very few who lived nearby interested in meeting Him?

I like church...but it bothers me deeply that God's people have so little influence on society. Can't we do a better job of capturing the hearts of the people in our communities?

Well, you don't need to feel sorry for Pastor Bob. His congregation has grown four- or fivefold in recent years and is now one of the largest churches in the Midwest. When Bob wonders whether the community is uninformed and unimpressed by the church, he's not just musing about his situation, but about 400,000 churches throughout North America.

Bob wishes, however, that his church ministered in a way that truly captured the hearts of the people in his town. Most of us have a similar longing, don't we? Wouldn't you like the people where you live to feel good about your church and the role it plays in your town or city? How wonderful that would be for the cause of Christ worldwide!

Researcher George Barna reports that in the coming year only seven percent of the non-churched will sample what's available to them. Another one-third might consider trying out a church under the right circumstances, but six out of ten non-churched adults state they are unlikely to visit a church in the next 12 months.[1]

Don't put too much stock in those unnerving numbers. The future of the church will be full of surprises, just as the past has been. So while I could be discouraged, actually I'm excited by what is happening in many churches today.

Since the beginning of time, God has been in the business of making contact with hard-to-reach people. He's won them over by ones and twos, by families, by cities, and by nations. Maybe Jonah had read the surveys, and was sure that not six out of ten, but ten out of ten Ninevites didn't want anything to do with his God. "Stop saying it can't be

---

1. George Barna, *Evangelism That Works* (Ventura, CA: Regal Books, 1995), 68.

done," the Lord told Jonah. He wanted His prophet to think bigger than reaching one or two, bigger than a Torah study group, bigger even than a mega-synagogue. God wanted to capture a great city with His love and grace. Nineveh was a cruel place given to prostitution, witchcraft, and corrupt business practices (see Nahum 3). But guess what? In a 40-day window of time, "the Ninevites believed God," saying, "Let everyone call urgently on God. Let them give up their evil ways and their violence" (Jonah 3:5a, 8b).

The Midwest weather indicators for January 26, 1967, called for scattered snow flurries. Meteorologists said the atmospheric conditions weren't right for a major snow. Yet that night the Great Lakes region was overwhelmed by the all-time record 24-hour snowstorm.

When God wants to capture the heart of a city, He doesn't pay much attention to the indicators. Church surveys may report that spiritual conditions aren't right for revival. But I believe cities stand ready for Nineveh-type miracles.

Building Bridges

A prevailing practice in the Jewish religious culture was that of building societal walls. Jews segregated themselves from non-Jews, men distanced themselves from women, the "righteous" erected invisible walls to avoid contact with "sinners," and the healthy lived separated from lepers and other diseased persons.

In politics we call this *protectionism*. Confident nations want free and open trade, while the nation with economic fears puts up trade barriers. A carefree America welcomes immigrants. An apprehensive USA listens to the voices that call for walls to keep newcomers out.

Jesus angered as many as He delighted by His practice of breaking down protectionist walls to build bridges to community residents. Levi, better known as Matthew, was not popular. As a tax collector, he was considered a traitor to the nation, abusive to widows and the poor, a man corrupted by a lust for money. Jesus built a bridge to Levi, and the tax collector "got up, left everything and followed Him" (Lk. 5:28). Don't get the idea that Levi just followed Jesus down the street. He followed Jesus right out of corruption and into discipleship. It was a lifetime of following.

Levi wanted his friends to meet this Jesus who had crossed over a bridge into his world, so he prepared a banquet for a large crowd of fellow tax collectors. To realize how unusual this was, I like to picture these guys wearing black shirts and white spats—the Mafia look of the Roaring Twenties.

Maybe that helps explain why the superpious Pharisee wall-builders complained, "Why do You eat and drink with tax collectors and 'sinners'?" Jesus had a ready answer: "It is not the healthy who need a doctor, but the sick. I have not come to call the righteous, but sinners to repentance" (Lk. 5:30-32).

Was it at Levi's dinner that the man we read about in Luke 18 began his spiritual pilgrimage? This tax collector stood at a distance. He would not even look up to Heaven, but beat his breast and said, "God, have mercy on me, a sinner" (Lk. 18:13). Who can say what prompted his search? But we do know that a bridge to the tax collectors had been built, and now these "untouchables" considered Jesus a friend and began to listen to what He had to say (see Lk. 15:1).

Banquets continue to be common bridge builders to the non-churched. Congregations use the "Levi method" when they host pancake breakfasts, Mother's Day dinners, Valentine banquets, block parties, family game nights, and Thanksgiving feasts. Individuals can build these bridges in their homes through hospitality and an agenda of friendship.

We can also build bridges to the community with events that make holidays unique. My family is annually touched by a Christmas musical produced by Ginger Creek Church. This drama, with multiple performances at the community college, treats a primarily non-churched audience to the beauty of the Christmas message. Live nativity scenes, Easter cantatas, and outdoor Fourth-of-July rallies can be community bridges. A Bethlehem bazaar might bring people into your building so that at least they know what it looks like inside!

My friend Chris Paul has a huge collection of baseball memorabilia. Churches invite him to exhibit his cards and curios as a bridge builder for local parent-child events. A sports clinic can foster interaction between generations as well as between believers and unbelievers. So the first step in capturing the heart of the community is bridge building. This is accomplished by finding ways to mix individually and corporately with neighbors, merchants, and even politicians.

From Bridge Building to Ministry

In addition to making friends with all kinds of men and women, Jesus went from village to village preaching the "Good News" while healing physical and social maladies. "The whole town gathered at the door, and Jesus healed many who had various diseases..." (Mark 1:33-34). The coming of Jesus was the hottest event in town. The head of Jericho's Internal Revenue Service climbed a tree to be able to see Jesus on parade (see Lk. 19:4). Our Lord completely captured the attention and goodwill of entire cities with His merciful deeds and words.

Recently I traveled with a group of physicians and preachers to India. Every day we visited a village with a medical team. A clinic was set up and free medical examinations were offered. The patient line-up kept doctors and nurses busy to the point of exhaustion. Following the daytime clinic we conducted an evening evangelistic rally. Huge crowds came to hear the message of the doctors and preachers. We were following the pattern of Jesus, ministering to obvious needs through loving acts before later presenting the message of God's love and redemption.

There is no shortage of ministry needs to which our churches may devote their time and love. Wouldn't it be great if we caught the attention of our communities the same way Jesus did?

During the Lenten season of 1989, First Church of the Nazarene in Bethany, Oklahoma, was in the midst of a 50-Day Spiritual Adventure. The pastor's sermons focused on bringing Christ's hope to the community. As members worked through a spiritual journal and practiced five spiritual disciplines, it was evident that God was quickening lives. At the end of the 50 days, leaders asked the congregation to identify community needs the Lord might want the church to be involved in.

They then summarized people's suggestions in 13 areas of potential ministry. These were published in the bulletin the Sunday after Easter with this invitation: "Look over the list of ministry groups, find the one that most interests you, and go to the corresponding room at 5 p.m. tonight."[2] Included were an adult tutoring program, Meals on Wheels,

---

2. Gary Morsch and Eddy Hall, *Ministry: It's Not Just for Ministers* (Kansas, MO: Beacon Hill Press, 1993), 85-86.

counseling for chemically dependent persons and their families, and ministries to the hearing impaired, to the hungry, to the homeless, and to those in prison.

Rather than processing everything through boards and committees, people were turned loose to follow the Lord's leading. The church staff would support where they could, but ownership and leadership landed on those with vision and calling. It was not assumed that all outreaches would prosper. People had permission to succeed or fail. Church members began to dream new dreams and experiment in new areas of outreach. An unemployment support group was formed. A RAIN (Regional AIDS Interfaith Network) team cared for one hurting man during his last days. Church members renovated the Bethlehem Transitional Shelter for Homeless Families.

Pastor Melvin McCullough learned that hundreds who received new spiritual energy during the 50-Day Adventure "needed an outlet for service and social action that would penetrate the community around us." He rejoiced "to observe a spiritual awakening that bore such observable fruit in transforming the culture and the community."[3]

Your ministry may be unique to you. Chuck Swindoll tells about his mother meeting a grieving widow in a cemetery. Swindoll's mom saw this woman weeping and

---

3.   Morsch and Hall, *Ministry*, 88-89.

talking to the marble tombstone, so she lov-
ingly, compassionately told her about Jesus
Christ. The widow's heart was open and tender, and she trusted Christ that day. This
widow adopted a graveyard ministry, spend-
ing her weekends at the cemetery ministering to others who talked to tombstones in
their grief. She led hundreds to Christ in this
innovative way.[4]

The Lawndale Community Church began
to thrive because of the effectiveness of their
initial outreach ministry. Their tools were
simple—a washer, a dryer, and a safe place to
do laundry. Honestly! Rev. Wayne Gordon,
Lawndale's founding pastor, was thinking in
terms of health care, recreation, and combat-
ting violence and drugs when he first sought
what to do. But as he listened, he learned
that what people saw as their primary need
was a Laundromat. "So we opened that
Laundromat," Gordon writes, "and people
came to our storefront church to use it."[5] This
was pivotal in the history of what is now a
great Chicago church and the backbone of
the Lawndale community.

We have not yet begun to push the limits
of creative ministry to touch our communities

4. Roberta Kuhne, *Seize the Moment, Share the
    Message* (Sisters, OR: Multnomah Books,
    1995), 52.
5. Wayne Gordon, *Real Hope in Chicago* (Grand
    Rapids, MI: Zondervan Publishing House,
    1995), 67.

with the love of Jesus. Steve Sjogren, pastor of the Vineyard Community Church in Cincinnati, Ohio, was speaking at a church in Houston, Texas, on the effectiveness of what he calls "servant evangelism." The idea was to teach people how to step out with simple expressions of God's love to outsiders. The last conference day was spent in the community putting this into practice—offering a free car wash, giving food to needy mothers, and other resourceful ideas that came to mind.

One group decided to preach in a park favored by joggers. To their chagrin not one jogger paid them any attention. Humiliation was added when the police ordered the church people to disperse. Defeated, this group began to slink off until one lady had an idea. She left for a few minutes and returned with 20 dozen popsicles. She figured that while the city officials required a preaching permit, they probably hadn't thought of a popsicle permit. This team soon learned that joggers who won't listen to strangers preach are completely open to talking to strangers offering them a free popsicle. Within 20 minutes all the popsicles were gone. But joggers lingered, asking, "Why are you being so nice to me? I don't even know you." The popsicle brigade told them, "We want to show God's love in a practical way."[6] Several joggers,

---

6. Steve Sjogren, *Conspiracy of Kindness* (Ann Arbor, MI: Servant Publications, 1993), 21.

intrigued by this simple act of kindness, took a running break to talk further.

Steve's church in Cincinnati touches thousands weekly with similar acts of kindness. Cleaning gutters, giving away Cokes, and even cleaning public toilets have proven effective ways to show the community God's love. The city has come to appreciate the value of this church, and the church itself has grown in a decade from 35 to 3,500.

Aurora, 40 miles west of Chicago, is regularly in suburban newspaper headlines because of a menacing drug subculture and frequent drive-by shootings. Its churches face the Jonah dilemma—shall we flee the city or try to show it God's love?

Love Aurora Sunday. That was the key phrase on a poster produced by the First Presbyterian Church. Pastor Dick Anderson and his congregation are committed to loving Aurora, though it is one of Chicago's most gang-infested suburbs.

On August 21, 1995, the Aurora *Beacon News* reported Mike Gerhard, Director of Christian Community Development for First Presbyterian Church, as saying, "It is in the spirit of John 10:10 that we host Love Aurora Sunday." In a large frame in the middle of the feature article, the paper quoted this verse: "The thief comes only to steal, and kill and destroy, I am come that they may have life, and have it more abundantly." These are hopeful words from our Savior to a troubled community.

"First Pres's" attitude of caring also encourages the city's infrastructure outside the church walls. The *Beacon* tells of a "Love Aurora Award" given to police chief David Stover. "Churches like First Presbyterian play an important role in developing community programs that focus on meeting needs of the neighborhood, like this church's involvement in God's Gym and the Wayside Cross Ministries programs," said Stover.[7] Interestingly, initial funding for God's Gym came not from the congregation, but from community sources. The recreation facility ministers to 2,000 kids above the age of 13, while Wayside Cross Ministries provides tutoring, Kid's Club, and Summer Day Camp. Church members are highly involved in both organizations.

Another feature of Love Aurora Sunday is the exhibits set up in the church narthex. Various programs are allotted table space for displays. Ministries such as Child Evangelism, The Salvation Army, and Riverwood Christian Center have literature and leaders to help answer questions. Community programs, including Adult Literacy Project, Crisis Line of Fox Valley, and McCarty Park Big Brothers, proudly show their efforts as well.

---

7. Amy Kolzow, "Church cites Aurora Police chief," *Beacon News*, Aurora, IL, Monday, August 21, 1995.

It was the consensus of the community-
sponsored programs that First Presbyterian
was the first church to show any appreciation
for their services to Aurora.

Did you note that Mike Gerhard's title is
Director of Christian Community Development? He oversees a team who works with
him. Winning Aurora's heart is more than a
once-a-year event; it is the church's year-
round goal. Gang members are being won to
Christ. Parks and neighborhoods are getting
cleaned up. "Go into all the world and preach
the gospel" is being practiced where Nike
rubber hits the court. The gospel of Jesus
Christ is gaining the attention of those who
are not likely to hear it any other way.

Mike and the First Presbyterian Church
do not serve in isolation from other churches.
Striving for attention, for credit, or for prospects has been all but forgotten among
Aurora churches as they unite in the "Prayer
Coalition for Reconciliation." These congregations are determined that together they
will transform their city. Intercession for the
city employees most affected by gang violence stands at the heart of this coalition.

"About 120 people assembled in North
Riverside Park...to pray for the city's public
and private school teachers."[8] This prayer
rally came two months after a similar rally

8.   Allan Gray, "DuPage overnight," *Chicago Trib-
     une*, Chicago, September 21, 1995, Sec. 2, p. 2.

for police officers. "Our prayers are with you, our support is behind you,"[9] said Pastor Don Hass of the Aurora Community Church to the city's law officers. The coalition sponsors a prayer vigil at the site of every homicide in the city.

Now when the press wants a story on anything from gang warfare to prayer, it goes to Mike Gerhard or the Prayer Coalition for quotable sound bites. These ministries have so captured the heart of the community that the press is reporting a turnaround for the good.

A Step From Ministry to Prayer-Evangelism

The church that wants to capture the heart of the community will begin with bridge building and continue with ministries that touch felt needs. But then that church needs to move into areas of prayer and evangelism. If we follow the apostles' model, prayer and evangelism should almost be one word—"prayer-evangelism."

All indicators suggested that Jerusalem was an unlikely place to plant a new religion, much less to establish its first church. Judaism was firmly entrenched both socially and politically. The Galilean disciples of Jesus had no power base. But after a season of united prayer, God gave them a special

9.   Gray, "DuPage overnight," *Chicago Tribune.*

anointing. When Peter stood to preach on Pentecost Day, the conversion of 3,000 souls was the direct result of this waiting on the Lord.

Prayer must be the forerunner of evangelism today, just as it was in apostolic times. An annual Pastor's Prayer Summit was concluding in Modesto, California. For four consecutive years the clergy had met one Monday through Thursday to pray for their churches, for their city, and for a mighty moving of God in their region. As the summit was wrapping up, a pastor suggested it might be time to attempt a community outreach. Another pastor mentioned that his church would be producing a gospel drama for three nights, and he'd be willing to expand this to participation with other churches. Since that was the best idea on the table, they all agreed. The drama, "Heaven's Gates and Hell's Flames," scheduled for three evenings in January of 1995, stretched on to play to a packed house for two months. Like an unexpected blizzard when only flurries were forecast, the response to the production was astounding. Thirty thousand new professions of faith were recorded in a city of 165,000! Churches baptized believers and conducted membership instruction classes for months. The entire city felt the impact of these prayer-led ministries.

Some congregations have neighborhood groups who visit homes and solicit prayer requests. Praying for neighbors builds bridges, ministers to felt needs, and enters into one of the highest levels of spiritual warfare. For instance, the pastors in a Colorado university city meet regularly to pray. Each month they invite a civic leader to speak and share his or her needs. These pastors, who have put aside jealousies and competition in their desire to win the hearts of their city, have witnessed dramatic conversions through the power of prayer.

Ed Silvoso tells of churches capturing hearts in Resistencia, Argentina, population 400,000. Seventy churches united in prayer for the city. Hundreds of intercessors were formed into 635 neighborhood prayer cells. Christians prayed for "the sick, broken marriages, rebellious children and financial troubles."[10] This praying, coupled with building water tanks in slum regions and conducting evangelistic rallies, touched the city's heart with Jesus' love. Within six months the church census had grown over 100 percent. Two years later the cumulative growth was 500 percent with 200 congregations, an increase of 130 churches.[11]

It is estimated that a million Christians fast regularly as they pray for friends and family members, for their churches and communities, and for another great spiritual

10. Ed Silvoso, *That None Should Perish* (Ventura, CA: Regal Books, 1994), 49.
11. Silvoso, *That None Should Perish*, 53.

awakening. Friday has become the prayer and fast day for many. Some fast weekly, while others fast and pray the last Friday of the month.

Whatever you do, prayer must be at the center of winning even one heart for Jesus, for only God can open spiritually blinded eyes. Prayer must also be at the core of any movement to capture the heart of a community, for the struggle is higher than the level of handshakes—it is a spiritual battle.

The hearts of our communities can be won. When Christian people build bridges, minister to needs, and unite in prayer, the power of God is released in unusual ways. Satan knows this. That's why Jesus pictured him as a wall-building protectionist, fearfully trying to keep his defeated kingdom intact. I see his domain as being much like the former Iron Curtain countries that slavishly kept their subjects inside and free people away. Jesus postured His church as aggressively assailing satan's ugly gates in all parts of the earth (see Mt. 16:18). The truth is, satan's kingdom cannot prevail against a bridge-building, ministering, praying, evangelizing church. And I believe this kind of advancing church, which captures the hearts of our communities, is something we all long to be a part of.

As I fly across North America I often see churches with their spires reaching high toward God from the very center of cities. Generations ago, when these towns were being formed, the churches were centrally placed, and often used for town meetings and schools as well as the worship of the Lord. Today's churches have generally been pushed from the hub of community life to the outer edge, all to be ignored and forgotten. In some cities the church is even considered a nuisance. At one time the church was the acknowledged heart of the community. Today it must reach out to capture the community's heart. I long for that for my church as you do for yours, and I see it happening in many places.

Cities are central to God's redemptive strategy. The Great Commission begins with a city—Jerusalem, and culminates when another city—the New Jerusalem—becomes God's eternal dwelling with his people.

> Ministry in its purest and simplest form is love. Ministry is, in fact, doing love.
> —*Win Arn*

❖ ❖ ❖

> I said, "Let me walk in the fields;"
> He said, "Nay, walk in the town;"
> I said, "There are no flowers there;"
> He said, "No flowers, but a crown."
> —*George McDonald*

Make It Happen

*These activities will help you begin
to capture the heart of your community.*

Individuals

1. *Host a letter-writing party.* Bring friends together—or sit down by yourself—and write your community leaders, town merchants, and local services to thank them for what they've done in your community. If you don't agree with everything a politician or business person stands for, find an issue or two with which you do agree and affirm him or her for those. Sometimes a supportive, appreciative note is all it takes to boost an administrative agency's spirits or encourage an officeholder to honestly serve your city. Go ahead and thank them—your efforts may produce even more reasons to be thankful.

2. *Play ball.* Take a break from your church sports league and join the community team. Really! It's difficult to capture the hearts of other community members if you're always playing *against* them, and it's even harder if you don't come in contact with them at all. Respectfully let the captain of the church softball or volleyball team know you're taking a season's sabbatical. (You might even suggest that the whole team make next year its "missionary term.") *Note to sports hotheads:* Be careful! Remember that you'll be representing the church—and Christ Himself—while you play in the

community league. Temper tantrums and legalistic nit-picking will not make a good impression on anyone. On the other hand, humility and servanthood will attract other players' attention. That's a great way to capture their hearts!

3. *Present yourself as Christ's servant to your town.* Of course you can't add a 20-hour-a-week community job to your schedule, but you can probably find time to be a once-a-week or once-a-month helper. Advertise your capabilities as a chauffeur for elderly people who need a ride to the grocery store. Pitch in on Saturday afternoons to ring up sales at the local goodwill resale shop. Offer to teach an Origami for Kids class with the city park district, or to tutor struggling students at the public high school. Whatever you're good at, whatever you enjoy, whatever resources you have, find a creative way to use those things to reach out to the people around you. And be sure to tell anyone who asks that you're doing it to show him or her God's love.

Families

4. *Create a Family Relief Team.* Take an hour in the evening or a dinner table conversation to brainstorm ways you could serve your community as a family. Set aside a specific time period—the 50 days between Easter and Pentecost or the three summer months, for instance—during which you determine to stick with a certain family ministry. You may decide to bring ribbon-tied

candy bars to patients in the community hospital, or deliver weekly hugs to residents in a convalescent center. (Elderly folks *love* to see children.) You might have your kids bake a loaf of bread in your bread maker each day during the week, then tote your "Family Relief Team" to the poorer side of town to give them away. Teach your family consistency in ministry—let this be an activity each member will look forward to doing together.

5. *Get involved in children's activities.* The PTA, Boy Scouts, or YMCA offer many opportunities for you and your youngsters to be in touch with the community. Encourage your kids to make friends on the Little League team—and learn from them! Common children's activities will build bridges between you and other parents. So make it a priority to be a ready volunteer for little Jenny's Brownie outings and a devoted fan at Joe's junior varsity soccer games. Your dedication to your family will catch bystanders' attention, and your interest in what *their* kids are doing will certainly capture their hearts.

6. *Make cheer-up cards for hurting people.* Is your boss anticipating back surgery sometime soon? Did the sad-faced grocery store clerk mention that she's going through a divorce? Sit your children down with construction paper, crayons, and stickers on a Sunday afternoon and let them create comfort and encouragement for the people you encounter

every day. Print across the front of the cards, "Hope you're feeling better soon," "Here's a little something to make you smile," or "I'm praying for you" (make sure you *do* pray for hurting people with them). Let your kids decorate the cards, then bring them along on your "special delivery mission" so they can see the smiles they bring to people in your community.

Churches

7. *Invite community leaders to speak to your congregation.* Although it's probably not a good idea to ask a civil servant to give the morning homily, he or she is likely to have plenty of experience in motivating people. So give the town mayor, city alderman, or school district superintendent ten minutes to talk about what is happening in the community and how your congregation can get involved. Your pastor may want to conduct an interview, asking questions like, "What problems are prominent in our community?" "How can we as a church help in this area?" and "How can we best pray for you?" Conclude by praying for the spokesperson and his or her colleagues. You may also want to arrange for a sign-up table in the narthex so that church members can commit to helping out where your civil leaders need it most.

8. *Open your church building to community activities.* Accommodate a Red Cross blood drive or make space for voting booths on election day. Prepare your nursery so that

mothers have a place to feed their infants and change diapers during the town carnival. Offer your church grounds for the Historical Society's annual Founder's Day reenactment, and allow spectators to use your restroom facilities. Let your church building—as well as your church people—be a servant to the community.

9. *Plan a godly holiday fling.* Isn't there a reason Christmas begins with "Christ"? Why shouldn't Canada Day, Labor Day, and other "non-religious" holidays be a time for the community to connect with God's family? The church is the cleanest, safest place for a party, and its people are the most joyful on earth. Show your community how to *really* celebrate! Gather the neighbors for a time of patriotic hymn singing and fireworks admiring, or invite them to participate with you in a Thanksgiving art show. (You can set up a gallery in your fellowship hall.) Even non-Christians are touched by special acts of courage, so advertise a memorial service for Martin Luther King Day, complete with a reading of one of his speeches and a moment of silence to commemorate the man of God. Don't keep your congregation wishing the bad aspects of a holiday would go away; instead, reclaim the day for Christ and His church.

3

I Like Church, But
I Wish Everyone Could
Feel Welcome There

Whoever comes to Me I will never drive away.
                    —*Jesus*, John 6:37b

The community church had worked to
maintain beauty and dignity in its worship
service. In this Midwest college town, the
rich tones of the pipe organ were considered
fitting rather than old-fashioned. Worshipers
often came early to meditate—and to secure
their favorite pew. That's because the sanctuary was frequently full by the time the service started. Sunday dress was still what
earlier generations meant by "Sunday dress."
Parents and children polished their shoes
and wore their handsomest suits and skirts
to church. They felt God was worthy of the
best they had to offer. These were long-held
community standards. But the college students came from various parts of the country.

Their worship habits were often more casual. And some students pushed "casual" to the edge.

Church was packed on the second Sunday of September. Vacations were over and the students had returned. When a sanctuary fills with friendly worshipers, it generates wonderfully warm feelings—unless you're someone who arrives a little late and can't find a seat. Skilled ushers are often the heroes on these occasions

Was it a freshman who entered the sanctuary ten minutes after the service had begun? Who else would wear sandals, shorts, and a T-shirt that read, "Visit sunny..."? (You might never know the place because it was tucked into his shorts.) He seemed to be dressed for the beach, but he didn't look ready for worship. Not to most eyes. "Thanks, bro," he said when handed a bulletin. Then he brushed by the usher to look for somewhere to sit. Glancing left and right, he walked up the center aisle and eventually reached the front row. Would you believe there wasn't a seat available anywhere? Tension mounted. Regular worshipers forgot their worship to watch this unseemly show. What would he do now? Would he crowd in where no space existed? Would he turn around and leave?

The student creatively solved his problem. He sat down cross-legged in the aisle between the front two pews. People's expressions could easily be read. What a lack of decorum. Nothing like this had ever occurred before. Is he just going to sit there through the whole service?

At the rear of the sanctuary, gray-haired Deacon Oakley was serving as head usher. From the time he was young, he had been taught to dress for church in the clothes he would wear to see Jesus. So he had on a blue three-piece suit and an elegant tie. A gold watch fob gleamed from his vest.

Oakley—his name was appropriate. He was old and strong like a tree. In previous years he chaired the church board, and his reputation was solid. People said, "Oakley's quiet, but he's wise." If anyone could handle the distraction gracefully, this man could.

Eyes turned to the back of the church as Deacon Oakley began to walk slowly down the aisle. On Sundays he brought a gold and ebony cane to support himself. His trek to the front seemed to take forever. Entire wedding processions had finished in less time.

When he finally stood next to where the student was sitting, the good deacon looked down and hesitated for a moment. Then he dropped his cane in the aisle, slowly lowered himself to the carpet, and offered a hand to the young man. In a stage whisper he said, "Glad to have you with us today." Then the wise elderly man and his young guest worshiped together right there in the center aisle.

Deacon Oakley understood that sometimes you have to extend yourself a bit to make sure a person feels welcome.

My eyes teared up when I first heard that story from Pastor John Casey. Then he preached beautifully about the many occasions Jesus surprised His disciples by the graciousness of His welcome. Pastor John was right. Christ went out of His way to make sure people felt at home, especially those who had known the sting of rejection.

Remember an occasion when you felt left out, ignored, or unwelcome? Maybe it was a family reunion on your in-laws' side. You sat unnoticed while your spouse's cousins jabbered about old times. It might have been the cool reception you got at your new job; people still preferred the person you replaced. Worst of all, it could have happened when you visited a church and were made to feel more like an intruder than a brother or sister in Christ.

Rejection hurts! It hurt when your date stood you up, or when the college of your choice turned down your application, or when the company you served for decades forced you out in a corporate downsizing. Maybe you still remember the sting of being excluded years ago from a circle of grade schoolers who decided they didn't want you as a friend. What grade were you in when that happened? How old are you now, and why is it you can still remember the pain you felt? Late in life my mother had similar feelings when she became a widow. "I'm not first in anyone's life anymore," she told me, feeling lonely and rejected.

A young friend invited a college classmate of another race to his church. His buddy seemed to be accepted. But as they were leaving, a church leader pulled my friend aside and said under his breath, "Don't you ever do this again. Not here!" May God forgive him. The place where rejection should *never* be felt is the church.

I long for churches of our land to be so welcoming that communities stand in awe because God's people are setting the standard for neighborliness and reconciliation. I pray earnestly that churches will welcome individuals from all strata of life, and that they will do it with joy and intentionality. Wouldn't it be marvelous to know that your church was thought of as a model for what it means to greet all people with open arms? With revival as a possibility, we can dream about the day when every church will reach out to all visitors with the warm and loving embrace of Jesus. It can happen, and it must!

Why Is Welcoming So Important?

The first impression people get of a church is its welcome. That initial greeting establishes feelings that are hard to ignore or overcome. "I liked the church, but..." is often followed by first-impression comments about the welcome: "No one spoke to me. I couldn't believe it." Instead it could be, "I liked the church because everyone was so kind and gracious," or, "I felt like I'd been welcomed by my family."

When I was a teenager, my folks moved and we needed to find a new church home. We visited a place where my parents already knew a few of the members. At dinner that Sunday it was time for the first what-did-you-think-about-the-church session. (Count on it—there is *always* a "first visit debriefing.") My parents' impressions were all positive. When my turn came, I complained, "I don't like the place. The young people are stuck-up. I want to go where they're more friendly." My parents decided we would try the church for six weeks, then make a decision to stay or look elsewhere. By the sixth week I had been given an important role in the youth group and couldn't have been dragged away. But I was surprised a month or two later when my new friend, Joel Ahlstrom, confessed, "Now that I know you, I like you. But when you first came, I thought you were conceited." How ironic—visitors make first impressions too! But the most important impression for Kingdom purposes is still the one the visitor takes home.

In the story of Mr. Oakley and the college student, you got a sense of the church's first impression of the student. What should have been important to every member was the student's feelings. I wish I could have eavesdropped on the dorm debriefing that went on later. "The place was so crammed I had to sit on the floor. But this neat old guy with a cane came and sat by me. I couldn't believe it. Why don't you come with me next week? I'll introduce you to him."

Jesus understood both the value of welcoming and the pain of feeling rejected. His welcome to this world wasn't the greatest. Other than Joseph and Mary, no one was right there to greet Him. Angels had to arrange the shepherd's reception party. Rejected by the people He served, Jesus died a criminal's death. But at the place of the skull where they took His life, He found time to welcome a lonely thief to paradise. Was it because Jesus lived His life more as a visitor than as a resident that He was conscious of the importance of always extending a welcome? Maybe it was just because He loves everyone. Then again, it had to be both. We will welcome people best when we love as Jesus loved, and when we choose, for the sake of others, to remember how much rejection hurts.

Whom Should We Welcome?

Cameron Townsend, founder of Wycliffe Bible Translators, is remembered for his genuine humility and his love of people. Nationality, race, wealth, education, status— none of these influenced how Mr. Townsend welcomed people. Billy Graham wrote of Cameron, "He had no flash or sophistication, yet he knew the presidents of 40 countries. Perhaps he accomplished so much because he showed the same courtesy to an Indian peasant as to an ambassador."[1]

The ancient Hebrews were reluctant to even whisper the name of God. The most holy place in the tabernacle was off-limits to all but the high priest. They were taught that God was so pure He could not look at sin. So it was risky to approach Him or His dwelling place in a casual way.

When Jesus came on the scene, the Hebrew faithful were confused. Instead of seeing themselves as unclean before a holy God, they had come to think other people were too unclean for them. Some were judged unclean because of their deeds, and others, like the Gentiles, because of their race. Women were impure once a month. Eating pork and other restricted foods made people unclean. Not many were left who were clean enough to approach God, and these few looked suspiciously at one other.

Jesus, who called Himself the Son of God, mingled with Gentiles, prostitutes, crooked tax collectors, and a strange assortment of unclean people. The crowds loved this. But it upset the religious leaders and threatened their authority. Nevertheless, Jesus treated everyone equal. The One who changed water into wine also healed the blind, the lame, and

---

1. Rev. Billy Graham with Philip Yancey, "Unforgettable Uncle Cam" *Reader's Digest* (September, 1986)

the lepers. As He welcomed the "less-than-pure," whole communities followed Him. People felt good about themselves after they were around Jesus. He favored people and this welcoming marked the entry of many of them into His Kingdom.

As Christ's church emerged, it continued to welcome everyone. In Jerusalem there wasn't a First Greek Church on one corner and a First Palestinian Church just across the street. All were welcome in spite of distinctives. The Jerusalem church, which exploded on the scene following Pentecost, was a bilingual congregation. The histories and holidays of the people were different. It wasn't always a happy arrangement, but they worked through their problems (see Acts 6:1-7). They didn't consider starting separate churches just because one person wore a sweatshirt that proclaimed, "Athens, the [heart] of the Olympics" and another sported a "Say *Shalom* to Jerusalem" logo.

This was not a homogeneous church. No one suggested building sanctuaries for people who shared a natural affinity—race or wealth or accent or artistic tastes. These people were called by the Spirit of Jesus to a supernatural affinity. The resurrected Christ drew them together and everyone who had been made alive by His Spirit was an important part of this phenomenal new family.

In the church at Antioch, Christians who came from a Jewish heritage worshiped and

served together with Gentile believers. But
old habits often creep back. When Peter and
Barnabas were in town, for all practical purposes they divided the church. Now there
was a Jewish Christian sector and a Gentile
Christian sector. That's because Jewish
Christians felt a little squeamish around the
Gentile Christians, especially at the potluck
fellowships. Frankly, some said the Gentile
believers weren't clean enough. Besides, they
had different musical tastes and came from
different kinds of schools. So the Hebrew
Christians said, "We make a motion that you
form a church for people more like you are.
But don't get us wrong. This is only so you
can end up with a church where you're really
comfortable."

A church for every flavor and taste...it
might have seemed rational. But there was a
problem with this Baskin-Robbins approach.
Paul put his finger on it: "I saw that they
were not acting in line with the truth of the
gospel" (Gal. 2:14a). The apostle had a conviction that in Christ we are one reconciled
family. Prejudice was the height of idolatry,
because it worships self and those like us.
Prejudicial issues of any kind were impossible for God to bless. The church had to return
to welcoming everyone who came. Otherwise,
years later there would be White churches
and Black churches; big churches for the
wealthy and only storefronts for the poor.
There would also be too many stories in

which a Deacon Oakley wasn't present to do the right thing. If that happened, the church would be in one huge mess.

How to Welcome

Welcoming begins with a heartfelt attitude. "In humility consider others better than yourselves" (Phil. 2:3b)—because everyone has something to offer.

My children, now grown up, are still embarrassed by my habit of talking to strangers. I like to engage waiters and salesclerks in conversations. The kids roll their eyes back in disgust. "Why do you have to talk to everyone every place we go?" they complain. Undeterred, I know that whenever I reach out to someone I grow and learn. I've had marvelous discussions with people some might consider unlikely—taxi and limo drivers, for instance—and a few of these have ended in prayer sessions. I believe everybody out there knows something I don't know. They've traveled to places I've never been.

Recently I rode back from the airport with a Chinese gentleman returning from Korea. After a couple of minutes of silence, I asked where he was coming from. He opened up about his views on people and international cultures in a conversation I'll remember ten years from now. That ride was better than a college course on international relations! Everyone has something to teach me in some area. So it's to my advantage to welcome others into my life.

The place to begin that welcoming is with Christian brothers and sisters. The California pastors participating in "Pray Stockton" have agreed to introduce themselves to the community at large as pastors of The Church of Stockton, avoiding references to their denominations. Their church members do the same thing. Non-churchgoers are beginning to use the expression "the church in the city," rather than denominational or individual church names. The most significant impact has been on the image the Christians are beginning to have of themselves. They see "one church all over the city."[2] As fear and competition have been minimized, a spirit of welcome has blossomed. Pastors welcome each other's friendship, and members of different congregations view themselves as players on God's one team. The cross-pollination of ideas and experiences is thrilling.

I love the church I'm a part of. But I've learned to esteem every church better than my own, in the sense that every other pastor and church has ideas and experiences that can be valuable to me. I welcome these. I've spoken in hundreds of churches and denominational conferences in recent years, and I've grown personally with each contact, each conversation, and each story.

2.   Ed Silvoso, *That None Should Perish* (Ventura, CA: Regal Books, 1994), 244.

Within our churches we need to develop a welcoming demeanor. In my last pastorate a different family was assigned to be the "hospitality family" each week. This household prepared extra food for the Sunday dinner. During the morning service they would look for someone new—someone who needed a welcome—to spontaneously invite to dinner. First-time visitors would frequently receive a lunch invitation. All didn't accept, but some did. One hundred percent of our newcomers were impressed with our ready welcome. During those years, most visitors who came seeking a church home became a part of our congregation. But more valuable than the Sunday meal idea was its inherent emphasis on looking for people to include—to welcome as we would our Lord Himself.

Some people don't know what to say to visitors. They ask, "Is this your first time here?" Then their minds go blank. Here's a suggestion. Figure out what you like best about your church...the way people care for one another, the diversity of your congregation, the pastor's sermons being so practical, the terrific youth program, or the fact that your congregation has the best cooks in the county! Once you know you're talking to a visitor, say, "Would you like to know something I really like about this church?" Who's going to answer No to a question like that? Then, with a big smile on your face and with obvious enthusiasm in your voice, answer the question: "What I really like about this church is...." Just be careful not to go on and on. The effect on visitors is remarkable.

For first-time visitors, a welcoming church should be user-friendly. Regular attendees may know where everything is, so signs aren't important to them. But restroom and nursery indicators with arrows are as much of a handshake as the one extended at the door. Twice recently I've driven to a church and stood in the parking lot wondering where to enter the building. If it happens to a church veteran like me, then it happens to others. "Entrance" or "Sanctuary" signs should have been my first welcome. When you go on vacation, visit a church and record your impressions of what worked and what could have been more visitor-friendly. Then compare how your own church measures up.

Bridgeway Community Church, where I worship, has a pastoral team of an African-American and a Caucasian. This in itself is a statement of welcome to visitors of various races and cultures. Our previously all-White congregation now has a multiracial atmosphere in the pews as well as in the pulpit. We think it's great! Every Sunday is a foretaste of Heaven, in which "every nation, tribe, people and language" will encircle God's throne (Rev. 7:9).

When the church is prepared to welcome and bless people, the Lord sends more of His sheep to that sheepfold. When hearts are prepared to welcome others, the Lord has great adventures in store for them.

My backseat slumber had ended. The voices in the car were agitated. "This doesn't look familiar," said one college friend. "I don't remember going through this town before," said another. "Where are we anyway?" Our summer mission team had finished the season with a relaxing day at Yellowstone National Park. We drove there from Idaho Falls and had explored Jackson Hole and Yellowstone until we were exhausted. Our plan was to return south to Idaho Falls. I agreed to drive the second shift and had slept to refresh myself.

An adrenaline rush from the frenzy in the car quickly alerted me. We were on the right highway, but had traveled two hours north instead of south! A sign announced the city limits of Bozeman, Montana, and it was nearing midnight. A quick survey of the situation revealed that we were too tired to turn around and drive all night. As a group of three fellows and two gals, we couldn't risk the honor of Christ or the mission by renting motel rooms. I suggested we find a phone book, call a pastor, and see if we could be housed overnight. No one was comfortable with the idea, but nobody had a better one, either. The "you thought of it—you do it" rule was invoked, so at midnight I called a minister.

"Hi, my name is Dan Lupton, and I'm part of a summer mission team. We're supposed to be in Idaho Falls right now, but we got lost and we ended up here in Bozeman. We're looking for a place to stay and wondered if you might be able to help."

What would you do with that kind of midnight call? I don't know what I'd do. But this pastor asked two or three questions to establish the truthfulness of our predicament, then gave us directions to the parsonage. At 12:15 a.m., five tired students with no toothbrushes or changes of clothing, were welcomed like close relatives into the home of this marvelous couple. They readied beds, couches, and air mattresses. The conversation over a hearty breakfast the next morning made a lasting impression on me.

Looking back, I'm amazed at the welcome we received. These people accepted us when they didn't even know us. We were made to feel welcome even in the initial phone conversation. The husband and wife didn't know our doctrinal positions, the school we attended, the color of our skin, or our nationalities, but they said we were welcome at their home. Their hospitable spirit influenced five malleable 20-year-old students, even as it must have permeated their church. What an experience!

The Lord has great adventures in store for those ready to receive them. Somehow, they always seem to relate to people. So to have an adventurous life, I believe we must always be ready to welcome others. In his blue suit, Deacon Oakley may have appeared stiff and formal to younger people, but in his old body there beat the heart of an explorer. When he dropped his cane and sat down with that sandaled visitor, he was sailing in uncharted waters. He didn't know where his actions would lead or if they would be met with the approval of others at his church. But as far as he was concerned, there was only one right decision—to treat this guest in the Lord's house as he would treat the Son of God Himself. So he welcomed him as best he could, and no one in the church that day will ever forget that welcome.

A newly planted church had grown from 15 to 100 in a couple years. As a guest speaker, I faced a congregation with a number of people who were the Deacon Oakley age, a few young adults, and 30 or 40 teenagers. I guessed that only six or seven of these young people were connected to church families. So after the service I asked, "Why are there so many teens here? How did they connect with you?" The pastor's answer was simple and direct—"They come by word of mouth. Each has his or her story and unique set of needs. We have twice as many teens at our midweek youth nights. I don't know how to explain why they come. It may just be because we accept them and love them."

I thought of my neighbors' cheery welcome mat at their side door. Those things really convey a message! Jesus always had a

divine Welcome Mat out. He turned no one
away, and His personal warmth drew many
to Him. I was proud of this church for putting
out such a Welcome Mat for youth. And I
pray with great longing for an awakening of
love that prompts churches everywhere to
put out the Welcome Mat for everyone.

If the Statue of Liberty can beckon to the
world, "Give us your tired, your poor, your
huddled masses," then we should be willing
to say to God, "Lord, we'll begin with whom-
ever you give us."

To all who are weary and seek rest,
To all who mourn and long for comfort,
To all who struggle and desire victory,
To all who sin and need a Savior,
To all who are idle and look for service,
To all who are strangers and want fellowship,
To all who hunger and thirst after righteousness,
And to whosoever will come—
The church opens wide her doors and arms
and offers her welcome in the name of
Jesus Christ her Lord.

❖ ❖ ❖

Do not forget to entertain strangers,
for by so doing some people
have entertained angels without knowing it.
—*Hebrews 13:2*

Make It Happen

*These suggestions will help you
practice welcoming all people.*

Individuals

1. *Walk in a newcomer's shoes.* Visit another church with a different tradition or format from your own. If you attend a very formal worship service, visit a church that includes a lot of contemporary singing. If you're from an independent congregation, visit a church with a strong denominational affiliation. Or, if you're from a big suburban church, find a rural congregation to peek into. You may want to save this as a project for an out-of-town vacation or an evening or midweek service that doesn't conflict with your own. Whenever you do it, mentally note what made you feel welcome and when you felt most uncomfortable. Then use what you've learned to make your own church a more welcoming place for visitors.

2. *Go ahead, talk to people!* Each week, introduce yourself to at least one person who is new to the church, or just new to you. Be sure to reach outside your own circle. If you're retired, talk to a young mother. If you're a teenager, ask a younger kid some questions about himself. Just think—in a year, your welcoming committee of one can reach over 50 new people!

3. *Widen your margins.* Church days are busy times—speaking with friends, taking

care of weekly church responsibilities, seeing that the kids are picked up on time and the dinner will be ready when you all get home.... If your Lord's Day is so hectic you have no time to greet those outside your family or circle of friends, it's time to slow down! Try to unclutter your schedule. Avoid planning a regular activity or family obligation that causes you to rush away week after week. Transfer some of your "afternoon relaxing time" to "church time" so you can spend a few extra moments connecting with newcomers or those who need a friendly ear to talk to. You'll find the friends you make will be worth the time you missed relaxing— soon you may even be able to relax *with* your new company!

Families

4. *Adopt a family member.* Do your children think every adult is your age and has kids the same age as they are? If so, you need to expand their circle—and your own—by socializing with those who are different from you. Invite one adopted "extended family member" over to your home every month or so. You might choose a certain college student who'd love to take a break from books to play *legos* with your kids, or a single adult who hasn't been around children much, but could make an excellent "auntie Cookie Lady"! Seek out a surrogate grandparent, a foreign-exchange-student big sister, or a cross-town cousin. This is a great way to teach your kids

that people who are different from them can make the best of friends.

5. *Sign up to be greeters.* Have a plan for how you as a family can make newcomers feel comfortable at your church. Choose one family member to show new families where the nursery and toddler rooms are located. (Your kids should easily be able to do this.) Have another take visitors to a good seat— maybe one you've saved ahead of time. Give newcomers a quick tour of the church building, including the coatrack and rest rooms, and introduce them to several other people from your congregation. Be sure to recommend an appropriate Sunday school class. If at all possible, try to connect with visitors again after the service and invite them to come back soon.

6. *Play a memory game.* Often the "vital statistics" of a new person go in one ear and out the other when we meet him or her. The family unit offers an excellent tool for supportive remembering. Here's the way the game is played: Each Sunday family members look for someone new in the church. They must be sure to introduce themselves and find out about a visitor. On the way home from church, each one shares as much information as he or she remembers about the newcomer. The winner is the one who can remember next Sunday the most details about the visitors you all "met" the week before. Of course, the real winner is the new friend

whom your whole family will be able to greet by name when you get to church.

Churches

7. *Join in cross-cultural worship.* If possible, hold services with a church that is ethnically or economically different from yours. Worship leaders can each lead songs indigenous to their respective churches. Think of what a great choir you could have if choir directors combined their resources! Pastors can share the sermon, using a dialogue or interview format. Just look around your area for a congregation that is of another race or worship tradition, and try to work together. During this joint worship service, concentrate on inviting the others you meet into your social circle.

8. *Set up "name tag Sunday."* Ask everyone in your congregation to write out his or her first name and a few key words that relate a special interest or experience. For example, people could write "Traveled over Europe," "Own six cats," or "Have moved ten times." Encourage them to be creative, to come up with something interesting that those around them might not know. *Be sure to include visitors in this exercise.* Then, during the service or at a snack time afterward, explore one another's name tags.

9. *Eat 'round the world.* Introduce the church to their "extended family heritage" in the body of Christ by designating a different ethnic background meal for each

month—Italian pasta in January, Mexican enchiladas in February, Japanese seafood in March, etc. If someone doesn't have a strong ethnic connection, invite him or her to sign up for the month that sounds most interesting. Or, if one ethnic group only has a few people to prepare food, let them share the time with another group, assigning the main course to one, salads and side items to the other, dessert to both. If possible, play native music in the background and decorate your fellowship hall in a way that will give a cultural taste of the country you're celebrating. If anyone has an ethnic craft, instrument, poem, or game to share, allow time for sharing. As a conclusion to your monthly march around the globe, have a potluck dinner in which everyone brings an ethnic dish or a favorite food from childhood.

4

I Like Church, But
I Want It to
Empower People

Come, follow Me...
and I will make you fishers of men.
—*Jesus*, Matthew 4:19

"Just hope you don't get Miss Vandenberg for a teacher. She's tough!" My family had moved into a new house during the summer, so the neighbor kids were instructing me on the ins and outs, the dos and don'ts of my new school. One of the two sixth-grade teachers at Blackman Elementary—Miss Vandenberg— was a definite *don't*.

In late August a form arrived in the mail notifying me that I was assigned to Miss Vandenberg's class. My heart sank. It seemed everybody else in school knew each other— students and teachers, custodians and administrators. I not only had to deal with all the new-kid-on-the-block issues, but I also had to face the meanest teacher of them all. I imagined she'd be like Cruella Deville, the villainess of *101 Dalmatians*.

This new sixth-grade class was a month or two ahead of where my fifth-grade class had left off in math. In the very first school week I was bewildered when we studied decimal division. Miss Vandenberg directed me stay in from recess. *Look out now!* I thought. But she quickly brought me up to speed, and in that 15 minutes I learned decimals. I also learned that Miss Vandenberg cared for her pupils and would sacrifice her breaks to ensure our success. Although we had a well-ordered, no-nonsense class, I could detect no meanness in her.

Miss Vandenberg was as much a student as a teacher. She studied her pupils to discover their potential, and she worked to help that potential bloom.

As the second of three children, I was comfortably quiet. I could enjoy life without leading anything. When I played baseball, I usually chose right field and batted eighth or ninth. These were low risk positions in which I could do the least harm to the team or to my ego.

One afternoon Miss Vandenberg watched the class play baseball. The next day she took it upon herself to organize the game. "Dan and Joe will be captains," she announced. "Choose your teams and assign positions."

What a surprise! But it felt good to have the chance to lead.

The next day Miss Vandenberg again made me captain. This time I decided to play shortstop, a more skilled position. In the fourth inning the third baseman and I both ran to catch an infield pop-up. At the crucial moment we each politely stopped...and let the ball drop between us. Between innings, my teacher pulled me aside to ask why I let that happen. "I thought Mike would catch it," I said. The words *assertive* and *aggressive* didn't enter the conversation, but Miss Vandenberg taught me to go after every ball and not to assume someone else would catch it. I knew she was talking about a bigger field than a baseball diamond. She was coaching me for life.

Throughout the sixth grade, Miss Vandenberg called on me to read, debate topics, or go to the chalkboard more than the other sixth graders. The Dan who entered the sixth grade willing to stay in the background exited the class ready to stand up front and make things happen. Miss Vandenberg was my empowering angel. So many of her former students felt the same that seven years later she was chosen "Teacher of the Year" for the state of Michigan. That's a high honor for a teacher no kid wanted!

Other empowering individuals touched my life in the years that followed. Several were from my church. The volunteer youth

group sponsor, my pastor, church leaders,
and friends all contributed to unlocking my
potential. You probably identify with such experiences. Remember the people and conversations that were beneficial to you?

Most of us have a longing to be discov-
ered, to be given a better chance, to be empowered. "But where do I find someone to
help me?" we wonder. We all know friends,
cousins, nephews and nieces, awkward teenagers, even successful adults in the church
who long for further opportunities to learn
and grow and try new experiences. We dream
of finding someone who will believe in us and
give us that needed break. But stop. A better
route to follow is for each of us to ask the
questions, "Who remembers *me* as an empowering friend?" and "Does my church have
an empowering emphasis?"

Reflecting God's Empowering

Does God use men and women to build
His Kingdom, or does He use His Kingdom to
build men and women? The answer is yes to
both, with a priority on the people-building.
God develops people first, and in the process
the Kingdom is advanced.

In the Bible, when God called men and
women to a great task, they didn't respond,
"Well, it's about time You noticed my abilities—
I wondered when You'd get around to calling
on me!" That's because God has always seen
in men and women a potential that goes way
beyond what they see in themselves.

What is empowerment? *Empowerment is seeing what God sees in a person and helping it to blossom.* It's something everyone needs in life, and what better place is there to look for empowerment than among the people of God? Certainly our God is an empowerer. So my conviction is that the church we all long for will also be characterized this way.

That's the ideal. But in reality I fear too many people fall through the cracks. They're at church as a sixth grader, tenth grader, college student, young adult, 40-year-old, retired person, and elderly, and yet may have never heard anyone say, "I see great potential in you!" I'm afraid that in the church God's flowers aren't blooming the way they should. That's because we're not as good as we ought to be at seeing people through God's eyes.

God Empowered People Throughout the Bible.

When God called Moses to free the Hebrews, Moses answered, "Who am I, that I should go to Pharaoh and bring the Israelites out of Egypt?" (Ex. 3:11) Moses, who had been a humble out-of-sight shepherd for 40 years, saw himself unequipped for Jehovah's Egyptian rescue mission.

God brushed the first objection aside, but Moses had another: "What if they do not believe me or listen to me?" (Ex. 4:1). With his small bag of skills, Moses saw nothing but disaster ahead. "O Lord," he countered, "I have never been eloquent...I am slow of speech and tongue." (Ex. 4:10) Moses felt so inadequate that he finally begged, "O Lord, please send someone else to do it" (Ex. 4:13). Then the Great Teacher had to say to him, "Don't assume somebody else is going to catch a ball that's got your name on it!"

The argument of Moses wasn't that he was too busy for the job. His problem was that he honestly didn't feel prepared by life, training, or talent for this calling. Even so, God was about to make an 80-year-old Moses into a man much greater than he ever imagined he could be. First the Lord removed fear by assuring Moses that all his earlier enemies were dead. Next He made him a tool for performing miracles, and then He sent Aaron as a support to help with his speeches.

Ex 4:19

A grandfather followed these same three steps in his garage woodworking shop. A boy in the church, who could have been his grandson, had an interest in the lathe. But he was afraid of its power and didn't know how to start on projects. This godly gentleman invited the boy and his father to his workshop. He talked the would-be carpenter through his fear like God did with Moses, placed the right tool in his hand, and stayed next to him as he learned to use it, just as Aaron stayed with Moses. That's the kind of church story all of us like to read about—right?

Moses did more and became more than he ever imagined because God was equipping him, honing his gifts, and building his confidence. "Then the Lord said to Moses, 'See, I

have made you like God to Pharaoh'" (Ex.
7:1a). Jehovah was transforming this whim-
pering recluse into a man of great stature.
The runaway who said he wouldn't, couldn't,
and didn't want to "went to Pharaoh and did
just as the Lord commanded" (Ex. 7:10).
Christians and Jews all over the world still
look up to Moses. When God empowers a
man, it will take more than Charlton Heston
to fill the role.

God also saw a lot of potential in another
shepherd. We remember David as a mighty
warrior, an inspiring leader, and a gifted
songwriter. Isn't it strange that during
David's early years we have no record of a
family member or friend who spoke an encouraging or empowering word to him?

When a king was to be selected from the
sons of Jesse, all the brothers *except* David
were called in for consideration. Even Jesse,
his dad, didn't see many possibilities for this
last of his eight sons. David was too young,
too unassuming, and smelled too much like
sheep. He was just the family "gofer" (see
1 Sam. 17:17).

I wonder how many times today we still
overlook the potential of young Davids in our
churches. God even had to redirect the
prophet Samuel's thinking in this selection
process. "Do not consider his appearance or
his height"—those were errant criteria in
choosing King Saul's replacement. The Lord
reminded Samuel that "man looks at the out-
ward appearance, but the Lord looks at the

heart" (1 Sam. 16:7). Yet the prophet's memo on how David impressed him reads, "He was ruddy, with a fine appearance and handsome features" (1 Sam. 16:12). It sounds like Samuel himself hadn't learned to look at people through God's eyes.

I imagine somewhere along the line there were friends who empowered David. Do you think someone said, "You have an ear for music. I'd be honored if you'd let me teach you to play the harp"? Do we owe to this unknown benefactor some of the Psalms we have learned to love? Was there an observant shepherd who spoke up, "David, you're only 12, but you're growing into a strong young man. It's time you learned how to use a sling; you never know, someday it might come in handy." If so, that unknown coach changed the history of Israel.

God must have recognized that women in the Bible would respond well to His empowerment. After He announced the Christ child would be born through Mary, Mary spoke of her own humble or low estate (see Lk. 1:48). Because she lacked fame, power, or riches, she was bewildered that God would find her worthy of this huge honor. She lived in Nazareth, which means "sprout town."[1] It had the atmosphere of Western America's rough

---

1. G. Campell Morgan, *The Gospel According to Matthew* (Westwood, NJ: Fleming H. Revell Company, #), 19.

boomtowns that sprang up at the discovery of gold. Nazareth, an uncouth community, wasn't likely to have a finishing school that taught manners and refinement to a young woman made of pure gold. No, Mary didn't see this in herself. But God saw in her great wealth that just needed to be mined. Was Mary up to delivering a child far away from home in a stable that was hardly suitable? Could she flee for her life with her young son and live without complaining as a refugee in a foreign country? Had she the capability of gracefully raising an extraordinary lad? Yes! God instilled in Mary a poise and dignity that carried her through life, even to the cross where she watched her Son die. To this generation we call her blessed because the potential God saw in Mary was realized.

Jesus saw value and potential in people beyond what they saw or felt themselves. He put together a team of world-winners from men the Jewish rabbis said were unschooled and ordinary (see Acts 4:13). When Andrew brought his brother to meet the Messiah, "Jesus looked at him and said, 'You are Simon. You will be called Peter—the rock' " (Jn. 1:42, paraphrased). Andrew must have grinned, "Who's kidding who?" Peter would shoot out in unexpected directions like a wet watermelon seed from under someone's thumb! But Jesus saw enormous potential in Peter and committed three years of His life to the miracle of enabling a watermelon seed to become a rock.

Jesus saw productive possibilities in crooked tax collectors, women of the streets, palace servants, scholars, even a man who ran naked through the cemetery screaming. In every captive sinner He saw the potential to become a productive citizen of His Kingdom. Together they would someday accomplish greater things than He Himself ever had done (Jn. 14:12). Wow!

We need to develop this Christ-like habit of perceiving people as possibilities, not as problems. We need to check ourselves when we speak critically of others. We need to stop thinking, "I like the church, but it hasn't empowered me all that much." We need to tell ourselves, "I like the church, but I'll like it even more if I'm one of those who's empowering others like Jesus did!"

He Still Empowers Today.

"Single ladies work with women and children. They don't do church planting." That's the verdict missionary Marian Hovey received when she arrived in Japan a decade after World War II. Believing she was called to church planting, Marian persisted. She pioneered missionary television by teaching American cuisine cooking classes to reach women for Christ. She taught English classes to eager Japanese students. Those empowered with a new language through a kind teacher often welcomed Bible studies.

When a few women became followers of Jesus, Marian opened a Sunday school followed by a worship time. Men came on board too. A couple of weeks after a gentleman's profession of faith, Marian would suggest that it would be an asset to have him help with ushering. Soon she would request aid with Scripture reading or serving Communion. Both men and women grew quickly in her church.

Though Japan has always been slow to accept the gospel, the Lord allowed Marian Hovey the great honor of planting six churches and leading them to achieve self-supporting status. The keys to her success were many, including a life of prayer and a genuine love for people.

One clue to the Lord's blessing also had to be her humble approach to empowering converts in the church. Over coffee, Marian, now retired, told me, "I always explained to people that I was weak and needed them. I reminded them that I didn't have all the answers. We were going to serve the Lord together." Instead of being a controlling influence, she empowered those around her with training and freedom. While other missionaries had lofty requirements before a convert could teach, Marian was quick to notice gifts and encourage their use. In a natural, uncomplicated manner, she recognized potential in those around her, which made for a climate and structure for growth.

I love the story of Marian Hovey's life because it parallels the ministry of Priscilla in Acts 18. Both ladies empowered cross-culturally. Both accounts feature women empowering men. (Priscilla discipled and equipped Apollos for evangelism.) Both ladies also began churches in their homes that were characterized by a ministry of one-on-one empowering. These twin accounts involve missionary ladies who looked for potential rather than problems in people.

Even today, if a conversation about someone turns critical, Marian will always turn it around. "The Lord isn't through with that person. There's still a lot of time for her to grow up. You'll be surprised at what the Lord has planned for her." I'm 50, and Marian is still busy probing what I see God doing in my life. "Do you think you might try another kind of ministry in the future?" She won't let me coast. She's always there to encourage, nudge, or empower me.

Empowerment vs. Control

The apostle Paul was a most influential man in the emerging church. He was aware of the authority "the Lord gave us for building you up rather than pulling you down" (2 Cor. 10:8). Authority, to Paul, wasn't to be used to control people, but to empower them. He saw authority as a tool to help people become all they could be to the glory of God.

Dennis Bratton tells of a decision that set a new course for his church. The Mandarin

Christian Church in Jacksonville, Florida, changed its leadership style "from the traditional corporate approach, which seemed always to be asking, 'Who's in charge?' to what is called the Ministry System, which instead asks, 'Who's ministering?' "[2] The church no longer worries about who has the power to make decisions or give permission. The old system gave inordinate amounts of time to discussing what needed to be done, while the Ministry System invests the majority of time in profitable activity. When a system is politicized with high control issues, those with the greatest potential often stagnate. Given encouragement, training, and liberty, Christians will blossom far beyond people's expectations.

Unsure which church to visit, I picked up the Yellow Pages in the motel room and looked under "churches." It was the Saturday between Good Friday and Easter, and Nancy and I were 1500 miles from home. The church we chose was only seven years old, yet they were expecting 3,000 worshipers. Their sanctuary couldn't handle the Easter crowd, so they rented the civic auditorium. We arrived several minutes early and made our way inconspicuously to the center of the hall.

---

2.   Jeffrey A. Metzger, ed., *Claiming Your Place* (Cincinatti, OH: Standard Publishing Company, 1994), 21.

Seating himself sideways in front of us, a gentleman extended his hand in greeting. "I don't believe I've had the opportunity to meet you before. Are you visiting with us this morning?" I explained we were indeed visitors, but joked that we weren't likely to become members since the cross-country commute would be rather long. He laughed. His conversation was gracious and warm; then he departed looking for others to greet.

I was impressed, and more so when I opened the church folder and realized our greeter was the senior pastor. *With a full Easter program in a rented facility, why isn't he backstage reviewing final details?* I wondered.

The celebration began with a team leading the praise and worship session. The pastor didn't come to the platform. Looking around, I saw him at the rear of the church still welcoming delayed church members and newcomers. Public worship was neither pastor-dependent nor pastor-centered. The service continued with Scripture reading, announcements, a brief drama, and more jubilant Easter music. A children's choir came to the risers, and their performance was applauded. All had been led by church staff and lay leaders. Christ was glorified, and we sensed His presence.

When it was time for the sermon, the pastor finally went to the platform. He began by praising the children's ministry team that

had developed in the past few months. Then
he preached. I expected a pastor of such a
large congregation to be a mighty pulpit ora-
tor. I listened for a sermon proposition and
didn't hear one. "That's okay," I reasoned.
"There are many preaching styles." The message wound its way through an Easter text
and there were a couple of memorable illus-
trations. It was a fine presentation, but it
didn't account for all the Lord was doing
there.

After this glorious Easter service, Nancy
and I sat in the parking lot discussing what
we had observed. One visit isn't a full picture
of what a church is like, but I had impressions and I needed to sort them out. "I have
pastor friends who, in my opinion, have
stronger pulpit skills," I said to my wife. "But
their churches are a tenth of this church, and
they aren't growing. The strength of this
church is people power. This pastor's effectiveness is his dedication to empowering his
people to be all they can be. If there is a tension between control and empowerment, he
leans toward empowerment, and I think he's
wise."

He was not only wise, but he followed the
model of Jesus.

Jesus' plan from the beginning was to
have ministry pass from His hands to others.
He would build the church by building people. He would fill them with Himself and then
step out of the way. What began with Jesus'

preaching, healing, and teaching, moved on to the disciples' traveling from town to town preaching, healing, and teaching. The disciples then reported to their teacher for debriefing and further instruction. After three years Jesus left the scene with directions for His followers to continue the preaching and training process until every nation and tongue had been reached with His gospel. He didn't handle the authority issues by maintaining executive power over every decision, but by instilling His values, skills, goals, and Spirit in His followers. And He built a church even the forces of hell couldn't stand up against.

The Great Empowerment Adventure

I would be remiss not to mention that empowering is a delightful aspect of life. It's thrilling because it looks for the potential God sees. The cup is half-filled and moving toward overflowing. Perceiving people as problems is draining, but perceiving them as possibilities is invigorating. If Jesus had been content to evaluate Peter on the basis of the foolish things he said, Peter would have been kicked off the squad early in the season. But Jesus preferred to experience the joy of watching him become "hard as a rock."

Empowering is an adventure because we get to see people take new steps. I was a guest in some friends' home for a long weekend and volunteered to baby-sit while they went grocery shopping. Eleven-month-old Joel had pulled himself to his feet at the coffee table and was enjoying the living room view from this new height. I took his hand and helped him take a few uneasy steps. Then I thought, *Why not? Maybe he's ready to walk on his own.* With Joel balancing at the couch, I scooted back four or five feet, held out my hands, and encouraged him to come. The little tike must have been thinking, *Why not? Maybe I'm ready,* because he walked to me! Whether his glee or mine was greater, I can't answer. But we had quite a show to put on when Dad and Mom returned home. Although I actually had little to do with it, I always claimed I taught their boy to walk, and I felt good about this empowering experience.

Empowerment captures this same joy at any age. When I was 16, Pastor Stansfield let me preach a short message on a Sunday night. I don't know which of us was the most anxious before the service or the most pleased afterward. But my pastor had watched me take my initial baby steps at preaching, and he knew a father's joy! When you guide a teen through her first chicken Kiev and it comes out just right, who feels the most joy? When you turn over the Bible session to a new Christian and everyone says he did great, who feels the most joy—you or him?

We need to look for those arenas in which we can help others take new steps. Your story of adopting children might encourage and equip another couple to look into that same possibility. Cooking skills are not passed on as they were in earlier generations, so why not consider inviting a young person (or two or three) to an evening of cooking delights? Almost any skill or knowledge can be used to empower another's potential through a relational setting: resumé writing, growing a garden, caring for a newborn.... Empowerment is seeing what God sees in others and unselfishly offering your help in bringing that potential to life.

Let's reverse things. What if you see someone in your church with the obvious gift of hospitality, and you're new at the game? Easy—ask for her help in hosting a dinner party you're planning. Try public speaking. Learn fly casting. Get involved in drama. Master salesmanship. Take up photography. Work in hospice care. Experiment with metal working. Don't venture it on your own, though; get someone experienced to launch you into something new.

In *I Know Why the Caged Bird Sings*, Maya Angelou, one of our nation's renowned poets and authors, tells her story of being raised Black and poor in Stumps, Arkansas. Maya's parents gave her to elderly relatives who really didn't need another person to care for. The racially divided school system demeaned her by offering an inferior educational opportunity. Racism denied even basic dental care to African Americans. A neighbor, Mrs. Flowers, was the person who made the difference in Maya's life. She saw potential that others didn't see in Maya, and she was determined to bring those possibilities to life.

Maya was a fine student when it came to writing and testing. But she was mute in her classes. Mrs. Flowers invited Maya to an afternoon tea, which made her feel special in a way she never had before. Someone other than family valued her! At tea Mrs. Flowers explained that "Words mean more than what is set down on paper. It takes the human voice to infuse them with the shades of deeper meaning."[3] This tea was the first in a series of teas and "lessons in living." Mrs. Flowers (what an appropriate name) awakened in Maya an inborn love of literature, guided her to open up verbally, while disciplining her in a gentle discernment for life. As she taught Maya to recite poetry, she also taught her to "always be intolerant of ignorance but understanding of illiteracy. That some people, unable to go to school, were more educated and even more intelligent than college professors."[4]

This marvelous poet came to Wheaton, Illinois, recently on a lecture tour. I called for tickets as soon as I could, but her appearance at the community college arts center was already sold out. Maya Angelou has become a

3. Maya Angelou, *I Know Why the Caged Bird Sings* (1969; reprint, New York: Bantam Books, 1993), 81.

4. Angelou, *I Know Why*, 81.

literary hero for many Americans. But if it weren't for Mrs. Flowers, it's unlikely that any of us would know her name.

You and I are called by God to be the empowering Mrs. Flowers or Marian Hovey or Miss Vandenberg in others' lives. What a joy this is! It's part of what being the body of Christ is all about. And it's the whole body that is the answer; we can't expect pastors to empower everybody. God intends that all people who make up the church will be His empowering agents.

So yes, look for those who can help you become all God wants you to be. But also look for those who need help from you. Pray that what you learn about empowerment will spread. Pray also that before too long Christ, through His new body, the church, will again do what He did so effectively when He was here—empower people to become all God intended them to be.

It is a luxury to learn,
but the luxury of learning is not to be compared
to the luxury of teaching.

❖ ❖ ❖

Hold on to instruction, do not let it go;
guard it well, for it is your life.
—*Proverbs 4:13*

❖ ❖ ❖

Those having torches will pass them on to others.
—*Plato*

Make It Happen

*These suggestions will help you
learn to empower others.*

Individuals

1. *Play "I Spy."* Watch for times when people you know are really feeling good about what they're doing. Perhaps you've noticed a teenager whose face simply glows while singing in the choir. Or maybe you've run into a friend who is delighted to be picking out flowers for the altar, or a neighbor who is all excited about his plans for a woodworking project. When you see people who look joyful, talk to them about it. Ask why they feel good about what they're doing, when they first became interested in the activity, and what other things they might enjoy as well. Affirming and prolonging the joy others experience is a simple way to empower, and knowing what "turns their crank" may provide more opportunities for you to enable them.

2. *Put yourself "underneath" someone.* Rather than acting as a "high and mighty teacher" to those you empower, get creative! Let yourself be a stepping stone. Here's an example: If you work in the church nursery and see a junior high student who seems to like children, encourage him or her to join you—after taking a Red Cross baby-sitting class. Talk to the student's parents, offering to give their teenager a ride to the class. Your service will provide you with a first-class

helper, and you may discover some awfully fun company in the process.

3. *Share the wealth.* If you have an ability or talent others can learn from, don't let yourself get stuck in a coaching role. Find other people who share those same strengths so you can enable others even when you're not available personally. If you're good at music but can't take on any more students, think of other good teachers you might be able to recommend. If you're a writer but don't have enough time to teach your craft, make a list of classes or seminars you would endorse. By keeping a current directory of references rather than trying to do everything yourself, you'll avoid burnout. You'll also empower others who have similar skills—and who are interested in sharing.

Families

4. *Affirm, affirm, affirm!* Did you ever hear the story about the duck who was an excellent swimmer but a very poor runner? At school the duck's teachers concentrated all their effort on improving his running skills so that by the time they were done, he had pulled his running up into the average range. But, of course, he also became just an average swimmer because he had damaged his webbed feet. Sometimes we well-intentioned parents concentrate on our ducklings' running when we should be applauding their swimming. This week, take the time you usually spend correcting your kids' weak skills

(*whatever* they may be) and put it into enjoying something your child already does well.

5. *Hold an observation celebration.* Declare the next seven days "International Observation Week." Ask each family member to carefully watch the others to see what they are especially good at. Look for things that aren't too obvious: your teenager may have excellent telephone manners, or your six-year-old may be good at organizing his drawers. Give everyone a pad or a clean sheet of paper as their "observation notebook." At the end of the week, talk about the skills each person has spotted, and look for ways to put them to use. The child who can read in the car without getting sick might have the privilege of sitting up front reading the map on your next car trip. Or the teenager who is good at cooking may choose a menu and make the family dinner once a week. Remember, this should be an opportunity to empower, not to add chores!

6. *Create a family incubator.* Each person in the family should choose a talent, skill, or quality he or she would like to incubate. Remind everyone that, like an egg, this quality must be nurtured and kept warm in order for it to grow and come to life. They may have gifts of hospitality, but unless they visit the neighbors or invite others to dinner, that talent will waste away. Each time a family member uses a chosen quality or spends time practicing a skill, he or she will receive a

point (called a "growth spurt"). Finding a way to affirm or "egg on" a talent in another family member gains a bonus point. At the end of the specified time period, measure "growth spurts" to see who is tallest.

Churches

7. *Offer summer internships.* Hire a young person studying education to help lay leaders organize Vacation Bible School. Enlist a music student to work with the choir director in planning a special concert series. A business major might work with the pastor or finance committee to organize church records; a computer major could research a new church computer system; a beginner in the publicity field might write and set up the church's fall funding campaign. By allowing for an "internship margin" in your budget, you'll find beneficial skills from within your own congregation to help your church. This is also a great way to encourage young people to work with older believers, integrating what they are learning with practical Christian service.

8. *Bring folks together in like groups.* The church should be an ideal place to network. Look for those with similar needs and concerns who can strive toward a common goal. For example, those who are looking for a new job could connect on a Saturday to rework and critique their resumés. Young moms could meet for coffee to share questions and concerns on being better parents. Those who

are applying for college could get together to go over applications and discuss the pros and cons of the schools they're looking into. Whenever possible, invite someone with experience to join these groups (a personnel director, an older mother, a college admissions director). The support you'll find in these "communities" will help each member achieve success.

9. *Hold a gift exchange.* This isn't a Christmas-in-July exchange, but a swapping of talents and abilities. Set boxes on a table in your narthex or fellowship hall. Label each box with an area of giftedness (arts/crafts, hospitality/friendliness, teaching/education, communication, mechanics...). Try to group things together so your gift table is not overburdened with boxes. Supply paper so church members can stop by the table and write down something they're good at: "My homemade spaghetti sauce is out of this world," or "I can write a good 15-minute presentation in 5 minutes!" Have each person include his or her name, address, and phone number, then place the sheet of paper in the appropriate box. The next week, direct congregation members looking for empowerment to stop by the gift-exchange table and draw out a name of someone who might help them, then take their "personal empowerer" information home to make contact during the week. This can start a wonderful congregational

interchange in which both "sharers" and "benefitters" will be empowered.

5

I Like Church, But
It Must Model Integrity

*...Let your light shine before men,
that they may see your good deeds
and praise your Father in heaven.
—Jesus, Matthew 5:16*

" 'Fairy tale princess story' turns sour after newlyweds lose money." That headline story commanded the attention of millions in Chicago. A newlywed couple, driving away from their wedding reception, left a zippered black case with all their wedding gift money—nearly $12,000—on the roof of the bride's car. By the time they reached home, of course, it was gone. Vanished. "I feel numb—that's a good word for it. Overwhelmed," the bride said.[1]

---

1. " 'Fairy tale princess story' turns sour after newlyweds lose money," *Daily Herald*, February 20, 1996, sec.1.

Two days later, the paper shouted this headline: "Finder's keepers? Not all believe it." David Yi, an unemployed suburban resident, found a bag with about $12,000 in cash and checks. With all his bills adding up, he might have kept the money. Who would have known the difference? But his conscience wouldn't let him. He found the newlyweds and returned both their property and their hopes. David Yi hadn't considered keeping the cash. "I guess it doesn't matter whether it's $50 or $1,000 or $1 million," he said. "It doesn't belong to you. It's just right from wrong."[2]

The proverb "The integrity of the upright guides them" (Prov. 11:3a) proved true with David Yi. What would you do if *you* were out of work and one day happened to find enough to pay the rent for a month or two? Some might be tempted to consider it a gift from Heaven! Not David Yi. He was more interested in doing what was right.

Apparently there is a market for unemployed men and women with integrity. David has received job offers from Motorola, Ameritech, Sony, Hilton Hotels, and a Hyundai dealer who wanted to give him an office and a company car. It's all been quite perplexing for David Yi. The telephone has been

2. "Finders keepers? Not all believe it," *Daily Herald*, February 22, 1996, sec. 1.

ringing off the hook. "It's just bizarre, bizarre, bizarre," he said.[3]

To a man with integrity, it is peculiar that an act of honesty should be fussed over. To a news and business world witnessing so little integrity, David Yi's behavior was refreshing.

There is also a market for churches, large or small, that model integrity. The church you love, or will love, is marked by spiritual and moral integrity in its members and especially its leaders. Yes, such churches exist, and more are developing. The Spirit of God is affirming that integrity is His call for us today; nothing less will be acceptable.

Integrity breakdowns are devastating to church members and religious seekers alike. When a person leaves his church because of hurt feelings, he usually finds another church home quickly. But when someone drops out because of moral failures in church leadership, the recovery time is much longer. In these cases it is not feelings, but faith itself, that is under attack. The questions after observing integrity breakdowns are not "Where will I fit in better?" but "Can I ever again trust Christian leadership?"

"I once liked church, but I don't know whom to trust" is the thought harbored in too many hearts today. I long for that to be set right. I long for the names "pastor" and

3. "Man gets offer of jobs after cash returned," *Daily Herald*, February 22, 1996, sec.1

"worship leader" and "elder" and "deacon" to resonate with admiration whenever they are spoken. I long for the Christian in the workplace to be trusted above everyone else. A high school teacher told me, "Dan, society can function as long as ninety percent of the people can be trusted ninety percent of the time." That standard may work for society, but it won't work for the church. The church that can be trusted only 90 percent of the time can't be trusted at all. You know it, and I know it, but your non-Christian neighbors know it more. Christ's people and church must become models of integrity.

What Do You Mean, "Model"?

Many young women and men dream of being a model. Walking the runway in the latest fashions, appearing in catalogs and videos, or being the cover girl for a glamour magazine is the model's ambition. But Christians have a higher calling than the fashion modeling industry. We are to model life as it should be lived. We must attract others to the good news of Christ as living billboards of that good news. We model integrity so others may emulate our lives.

David Yi is one model of integrity. Wilbur Powell is another.

Wilbur Powell taught my Sunday school class in the 1960's, when I was in high school. As a young man in his twenties, he came to faith in Christ in a tuberculosis sanitarium. Those were rough years that Mr. Powell never spoke about unless we inquired. Fifty or 60 years ago, a TB sanitarium was much like a leprosarium or an AIDS ward. Tuberculosis victims were isolated from the public, and death was the common lot. People entered a sanitarium with a similar attitude to how you might enter death row: There was some hope of a reprieve, but you'd better be prepared to die.

The Lord brought Mr. Powell through that time with one functional lung and a heart full of faith. Friends in the sanitarium died while he was there. He viewed his healing as a miracle, an act of God. It was a holy experience with a holy God who was not to be taken lightly.

It amazes me that he was skilled in teaching high school students, because he'd never learned the latest teaching techniques. He stayed with the basic lecture method and occasional markings on a blackboard. His power was his thorough preparation and obvious love for God's Word, his life of prayer that brought the Spirit of God to the classroom, and the force of his consistent integrity. He never knew it, but the greatest lesson he taught us was what he had become.

We remember Mr. Powell for his *moral integrity*. He married his sweetheart and stayed devotedly with her until death took him. In their sixties, the Powells still walked arm in arm in public. He never jested about moral issues. Marriage and sexuality were sacred delights. High schoolers could learn much about purity and trust from just watching him.

Wilbur Powell was known for *integrity of word.* He spoke positively of God, of life, and of others. Your reputation was not only safe with him; it would probably improve when he spoke about you! His words reflected faith in God and faith in the people his students were becoming. Without flattery and without excess, Mr. Powell always greeted us in an uplifting and encouraging way.

One day it occurred to me that Mr. Powell had never served on the church executive board. I asked my parents about this injustice. They told me that my Sunday school teacher was not in complete harmony with the church doctrinal statement regarding a point of eschatology. The church was confident of God's end-time process; Mr. Powell had room in his mind for other possibilities.

My admiration for him grew. He wouldn't compromise in doctrine to obtain an office. Yet he understood this doctrine was not essential enough to cause him to leave the church. Indeed, he remained an enthusiastic supporter of our church. "How good and pleasant it is when brothers live together in unity" (Ps. 133:1), particularly if they don't agree on every issue.

I saw *financial integrity* in Mr. Powell. He was held in high esteem by civic organizations because of his monetary wisdom. It was my impression that he was doing well at business, yet simplicity marked the way the Powells lived. I suspect that since he faced death daily as a tuberculous patient, life and love were precious enough. Luxury items neither impressed nor appealed to him. He was a true Christian gentleman, serving his clients without taking advantage of them. He became a model of integrity for scores of young men and women in our church.

His *personal integrity* was priceless. Mr. Powell was considerate, kind, and—I believe—quietly generous. He gave gifts, supported missionaries, and dressed modestly. When he taught our class, I remember focusing on his face, his eyes, his kindness. He cared for us, and teaching us was an honor.

We grew under him. When Mr. Powell entered the classroom Sunday mornings, we were no longer just teenagers, but young adults, real people. He treated us as peers, although he was 60 and we were 16. So to learn from him, we came up to his level. We put away childish things in our eagerness to be like our teacher.

What did we learn? I can't remember what he taught us with words. I only remember the man, the model, the consummate Christian gentlemen, Mr. Integrity, Wilbur Powell. He didn't know he was my model and hero. But I still treasure the cut-glass salt-and-pepper shakers he gave Nancy and me at our wedding. The sight of them keeps him alive in my memory.

From that Sunday school class have come many businessmen and women, teachers, homemakers, international evangelists, missionaries, pastors, scientists, artists, and one U.S. Senator, Dan Coates. What did Wilbur Powell look like? He stood tall, straight, and dignified, much like Senator Coates. How did he speak? He spoke with intelligent, subdued passion, like Senator Coates. All of us in that class have become, in some measure, like our teacher and model.

Mr. Powell wasn't the only model of integrity in our church. There were many. The church itself modeled integrity, due to the men and women committed to its high reputation, to each other, to the Lord, and to His service. I feel fortunate; many churches aren't so competent in this area. But they can be.

What Is Integrity?

It is difficult to show integrity if you don't understand what integrity is and how it is produced. The biblical concept of integrity comes from a Hebrew word that means simple, whole, sound, unimpaired, or complete.

A quilt has integrity when its pieces fit tightly together with all the seams intact. It is *simple* in that it is one quilt, *whole* because no squares are lacking, and *sound* due to the tight seams. A car is said to have integrity when all its parts fit tightly in place and in original condition, with no hidden rust secretly devouring its underbody. A tree has integrity when its roots, trunk, branches, and fruit are healthy and fully functioning with sap from the roots nurturing the fruit at the tips of the branches.

Imagine a healthy tree as a picture of healthy Christian integrity. We are rooted in our faith, made upright by our values, which branch out to our actions. The fruit is our character. Many years ago I heard a radio preacher suggest, "*Character* results from repeated *acts of conduct*, which are guided by our *values*, which spring from our *faith system*." If our tree has integrity, the fruit will be sweet.

We model integrity when character, daily deeds, the values we claim, and the faith we affirm are joined together in a simple, complete, unbroken life system. Hypocrisy sets in when deeds and character do not correspond with the faith and values we claim. Let's look at this more closely.

Good Deeds Form the Fruit of
Good Character

Like tomatoes ripening over time, character develops as we grow. Your repeated actions will reveal a certain consistency, which we call characteristics, or "character." A seventh-grade boy may be talked into stealing a candy bar at a drugstore, but he does not immediately become a thief. His conscience may bother him so much that he never steals again. (Yes, I'm remembering an incident from my youth!) But a junior high boy who regularly steals candy bars is characterized by acts of theft and will soon be labeled a thief.

Remember the story of David Yi? The media wanted to make him a hero for returning the thousands of dollars he found. But was that one deed in character with the rest of his life? A friend remembered that David found $50 a year before. He sought and found the rightful owner. David reported in a television interview that he would only consider job offers for which he would qualify without his recent fame. It seemed dishonest to accept a manager's position for which he wasn't equipped. David's famous act of honesty was no fluke. It revealed his inner character.

The church people you appreciate most will have characters you admire. Ernie Smith came to faith in the Lord in the hospital after his fifth heart attack. He joked that the x-ray of his heart looked like Swiss cheese. Some suspected his deathbed conversion wasn't sincere. But Ernie came out of that hospital to seven years of beautiful love and service for the Lord. He cheered up nursing home residents with regular visits full of laughter and hope. He took teenagers out for lunch on their birthdays, and they told school friends about their friend Ernie. He wrote poems of blessing for discouraged church members and accompanied the pastor to visit newcomers, shut-ins, and the elderly. His constant deeds of love and kindness united to form his magnificent character.

His compassion was infectious—others were eager to be like him. His church's character became one of love and mercy because Ernie and those who followed his example did what was loving and merciful. The community knew this church not through its printed mission statement, but through the character qualities of its servants.

As the consistent conduct of an individual determines character, so the deeds of the individuals within a church form the reputation of the whole church. You'll love your church when you can affirm its overall character.

Good Deeds Branch From Good Values

Our actions spring from the values we hold, like branches from the tree trunk. Ernie Smith's conduct revealed that he valued the needs of others over his own. Wilbur Powell's actions showed he valued students and their futures over position. What David Yi did confirmed that he valued honesty over money.

Jacob's son Joseph was a man of unflawed integrity. The Book of Genesis shows us how Joseph's values directed his deeds with such consistency that he developed a reputation of godliness and integrity. One of the Egyptian Pharaoh's cabinet officials was Potiphar, who bought Joseph as a slave. He was so impressed by Joseph's life that he "put him in charge of his household, and he entrusted to his care everything he owned" (Gen. 39:4).

Potiphar was apparently a workaholic, and his wife became lonely. She saw Joseph more regularly than she saw her husband. You can guess what happened. "...Now Joseph was well-built and handsome, and after a while his master's wife took notice of Joseph and said, 'Come to bed with me!' But he refused....'My master has withheld nothing from me except you, because you are his wife. How then could I do such a wicked thing and sin against God?' " (Gen. 39:6-9).

Integrity not only says *No* to sin once, but it keeps on doing what is right. Joseph's moral character wasn't revealed by a single *no*, but by the accumulation of *nos* to lust and betrayal, and *yeses* to chastity and loyalty. Although Potiphar's wife "spoke to Joseph day after day, he refused to go to bed with her or even be with her" (Gen. 39:10).

Joseph's character ripened from repeated godly responses that issued directly from his values. He valued his master's trust. He valued the marriage vows of other couples "to cling to thee alone, till death do us part." He valued righteousness over wickedness. And he must have valued his conscience over liberty, for he soon found himself in prison after being falsely accused.

Our deeds reveal our values. Why is the news media so hard on a television preacher who is found with a prostitute, while it winks at politicians who do the same? Because the Christian claims high moral values, while the politician may make no such claims. The media is showing the hypocrisy of preaching one set of values while living another.

Our Values Are Supported by Our Faith System

Joseph was a descendent of Abraham, Isaac, and Jacob. He had a heritage of faith in God. His father, Jacob, had wrestled all night with the Lord until he was blessed. So God was the root and foundation of Joseph's life from his earliest memories.

Joseph also had his own experiences with the Lord. God had revealed Himself by a dream in which Joseph's glorious future was foretold. He had protected Joseph from being murdered and had promoted the young man in a foreign land. Joseph knew he served a God of honor who keeps His word and a God of holiness who is repelled by sin. His values came directly from his knowledge of and experiences with God.

Joseph was rooted and supported by his faith. What supports your values? Take a look at your actions—especially the secret ones—and you'll find what you truly believe. If your faith is in a God of justice, you will value justice and conduct all your business affairs with fairness. If your faith is in the God whose Word can be trusted, you will value truthfulness, and what comes from your mouth will be trustworthy. If you believe God is love, you will prize love, and your family and neighbors will know it. Those who believe in a holy God will value what is pure and clean in their humor and entertainment.

Many educators are alarmed at the rapid decline of character and conduct in the youth of our land. Movements are under way to return value training to our educational systems. But values can only live where faith is nurtured, just as the tree trunk can only live if the roots are healthy. The problem isn't only the decline of values, but the turning from the historic Christian faith that gave us our values.

Why was Christ so patient with sinners and so impatient with the Pharisees and Sadducees? The lack of integrity was intolerable to our Lord. It's as if He shouted, "I like Judaism, but I wish its leaders walked their talk." Do you recall His words in Matthew 23? "So you must obey them and do everything they tell you. But do not do what they do, for they do not practice what they preach. ...You hypocrites! You travel over land and sea to win a single convert, and when he becomes one, you make him twice as much a son of hell as you are" (verses 3, 15). Strong words, aren't they? Nobody likes a church that doesn't practice what it preaches.

The church must accomplish what no other institution can. The church must teach and model integrity—wholeness of faith, values, conduct, and ultimately, character. Like a tree with rotting branches, the church cannot model integrity if its members or leaders don't practice what Christ taught. The way to show good character is by starting from the bottom up. "I will show you my faith by what I do," the church proclaims (Jas. 2:18). We must all participate in guarding its integrity.

What If Integrity Is Lacking?

USA Today reports, "Honesty is the best policy, but not for increasing numbers of teens and adults who are willing to lie, cheat, or steal to get what they want." The Josephson Institute of Ethics studied 11,000 high schoolers, college students, and adults and found that "37% of high schoolers say they stole from a store in the past twelve months, up from 33% in '93; 65% cheated on an exam, up from 61%." From collegians: "24% say they would lie to get or keep a job, up from 21%...47% of adults say they probably would accept an auto body repairman's offer to include unrelated damages in an insurance claim."[4]

The quilt is coming apart at the seams. The auto body is rusting. The tree is infested with bugs. The integrity model is marred and needs repair, beginning with the house of God. With the majority of the North American population calling itself Christian and 34 percent claiming to be "born again," the integrity of each person will impact our communities. Praise and worship from hearts of integrity is said in Scripture to be received by

---

4. "Cheating, lying on the rise," *USA Today*, February 23, 1996, sec. 2A.

God as a sweet smelling perfume (see Ps. 141:2). What He smells from many today is not so sweet.

Nancy and I were leaving for vacation. We packed our cases, unplugged the iron, left the appropriate lights on, locked the door, and drove away. But there was a problem. We had overlooked one detail—the garbage can in the kitchen. It was only half-full, but it contained some raw chicken parts. And we lived in an apartment building.

After a few days, other apartment dwellers began to notice a "fowl" odor that didn't go away. They called the building manager, whose detective work led to our door, and then to our kitchen. The offending garbage was removed, but we heard about it upon our return—again and again. We chuckle now, but our neighbors never did find much humor in the story of the garbage that made them nauseous.

Professing Christians whose character and conduct do not correspond to their values are like that kitchen trash can. They don't just stink up their own lives; they make the whole church reek. Their pollution doesn't have to be out in the open. The sin hidden in the kitchen behind locked doors over time becomes detectable.

Israel was so polluted that God left. Pastor Eli claimed to believe the Scriptures, but he grew fat eating juicy morsels that were forbidden for priests. His integrity had a hairline crack. His sons took the cue from him that religion was not a serious issue, but a luxurious living could be made from it. Under the guise of the priesthood, they lived immorally, "treating the Lord's offering with contempt" (1 Sam. 2:17b). After a while it was no longer merely an integrity crack; the entire building had collapsed. The presence and glory of God departed (see 1 Sam. 4:22).

Eventually the nation sensed something was wrong. They lost all their battles. The borders receded. The "congregation" was shrinking. A spirit of melancholic emptiness set in until at last the people "mourned and sought after the Lord" (1 Sam. 7:2).

Maybe your church is starting to long for a greater sense of the presence of Christ and His glory. What do you do about it? Take notes from the people of Israel.

Their preacher-prophet Samuel instructed, "If you are returning to the Lord with all your hearts, then rid yourselves of the foreign gods…" (1 Sam. 7:3). How does that translate to our culture today? Clean out all the garbage that is inconsistent with godly values. The Israelites set up 36-gallon garbage cans (or the Hebrew equivalent 3,000 years ago), and the people threw in all the foreign gods that came between them and the one true God.

This literally happened on a score of Christian college campuses in the spring of 1995. At Wheaton College in Illinois, students stood in line from early evening until 6:00 the next morning to confess and forsake the sins and gods of their lives. This continued for a week. They filled garbage cans with unwholesome videos, catalogs of covetousness, sports equipment that took attention away from worship, immodest clothing, liquor, unwholesome books and magazines, and other items the Lord nudged them to throw away.

"But I don't really have anything like that," you may protest. In Samuel's day, sins without a correlating physical object were confessed after a period of fasting. Confession was a verbal way to "throw out the trash." The fasting was a time of humility, brokenness, and heart searching. These were not shallow actions. Truly repentant people didn't say, "Oh, I see my sister is confessing, so I guess I will too." Rather, they mourned their distance from God and acknowledged their need of Him. They threw away all the obvious garbage in their lives, and then spent a day or two (or more) fasting and searching their hearts for anything they might be overlooking. It was like a spring house cleaning—rugs and curtains were washed, every speck of dust was cleared from the cupboard corners, and floors and baseboards were scrubbed and disinfected. It was hard spiritual work.

Along with confession, the people of Israel "drew water and poured it out before the Lord" (1 Sam. 7:6). One of the Jewish paraphrases reads, "They poured out their hearts in repentance to the Lord." This pouring was a sign of deep sorrow and humiliation over the spiritual pollution. The water reflected their tears and grief.

Because it takes more than tears and a heap of discarded garbage to cleanse one's life, Samuel took a lamb and offered it to the Lord (see 1 Sam. 7:9). That sacrifice anticipated by faith the day Jesus would die for all our sins.

Throwing away anything that contradicts the faith you claim to believe, that pollutes your life or takes your attention away from Christ, is a way to show Him you mean business and you're not taking Him for granted. That's absolutely essential to keeping your integrity.

The Lord is watching your life. Others, both inside and outside the church, are observant too. If there is garbage, it's time to clean house. Within the church, the integrity of David Yi should not be newsworthy. It should be the norm. Within the church, good examples like Wilbur Powell should be common in every generation. Ask God to make you a man or woman of integrity. That's the only way the church integrity model will stay intact. It's what we long for in the house of the Lord. It's what God so richly deserves.

Every life is a profession of faith
and exercises an inevitable and silent propaganda.
—*Amiel*

❖ ❖ ❖

Satan is perfectly willing to have a person
confess Christianity
as long as he does not practice it.

Example is the school of mankind,
and they will learn at no other.
—*Edmund Burke*

Make It Happen

*These suggestions will help you
to model integrity.*

Individuals

1. *Put yourself under arrest.* Imagine what might happen if you were put on trial for your faith in Christ. If someone wanted to imprison you for living a godly life, would there be enough evidence to convict you? Think about what the prosecutor might say to "prove" that you are Jesus' disciple. Could he or she find witnesses from your family, your workplace, or among your friends to testify that when you say you're a Christian, you really mean it? What specific actions could people cite to confirm that your values are the same as Christ's? Would anyone testify for your release because you're just like everyone else?

2. *Write God a letter of confession.* If there are areas in your past or present that don't live up to Christ's high standards of integrity, make a decided effort to confess them to the Lord. Write a letter to God, outlining some specific problem areas you harbor or acts you've committed in the past that do not honor Him. Write God a petition for strength to change and improve. If you feel you need to make something right with another person, write out specifics on what you'll do to change things. When your letter is finished, read it over and pray about it. Follow up on

what you've promised God you'd do to get rid of whatever is polluting your life. Then take your letter outside and burn it as a concrete reminder that God has forgiven you.

3. *Watch what you watch.* In North American culture the definition of integrity is up for grabs. The "role models" we see on television and in the movies, the newspaper heroes and the fictional characters who catch our attention, often make their choices based upon what is most profitable for them at a particular time. Take a week to police these hypocrites by critically observing the people you encounter on TV, in videos and films, in newspapers, magazines, and books. Ask yourself what effect their decisions have on those around them and on the watching world. What specific actions might show a lack of integrity? What do they do to prove good integrity? How does your life compare? What would you do in their situations?

Families

4. *Look in the mirror.* Spend a few minutes discussing, "When others look at our family, what reflection do they see? Do they see something that looks like Jesus, or do we look like polluted people?" Talk about ways that your family can better reflect God's holiness. Make a cross with clear tape or draw one with soap on each bathroom mirror. Throughout the week as family members get ready to go out into the world, the mirror will remind them to reflect God's integrity.

5. *Investigate good models*. Talk as a family about the people in your lives who have shown good integrity. Perhaps a grandparent or another relative has always been scrupulously honest in business dealings. Your kids might refer to a teacher who was always forthright and kind; you may point out church leaders known as peacemakers who exhibit the same high standards in the community as they do at church. Once you've chosen some good models, write them a letter. Commend them for the good integrity they've exhibited. Ask permission to imitate them and advice on what your family can do to follow their examples.

6. *Take the "Truth or Garbage" challenge.* Pop an integrity question to each other during this week. When someone says or does something that sinks beneath God's measure of truth, kindness, or righteousness, stop him or her and ask, "Truth, or garbage?" Try to come up with a biblical support for your position. For instance, if your eighth grader mutters, "My science teacher is a real jerk," a family member might challenge, "Truth, or garbage?" and then say, "The Bible says to be kind and compassionate to one another" (Eph. 4:32). If you get rid of a phone salesman by telling him, "We recently bought new aluminum siding," your six-year-old might contest (hopefully after you get off the line), "The Ten Commandments say you shouldn't lie!"

Churches

7. *Hold a "Caught You Acting Like Jesus" awards ceremony.* This is an especially good way to recognize those quiet, behind-the-scenes types who often aren't noticed, but who definitely honor God with their actions. Tell stories about how they were particularly honest in business dealings, how they humbly served other congregation members, or how they unerringly follow the speed limit. (Be sure to get their permission first!) Encourage your congregation to keep an eye out for times fellow church members represent Christ in the community—by returning too much change at a restaurant, showing restraint after a bad call at a softball game, or defending a political leader against gossip, whether or not he deserved it. Give a small gift or a special certificate as an award for their good example.

8. *Adopt an integrity motto.* Set out a few sheets of paper near your church entranceway, or slip a blank piece into the worship service bulletin. Let everyone know that you're taking suggestions for a church integrity motto—a goal you can all work to attain, something that will tell newcomers what your church is about. You may want to turn to Scripture to find your phrase; the Book of Proverbs is a good place to start. Collect suggestions in a basket near your church exits, then narrow them down to three top ideas during the days that follow. Next time you

meet, allow the congregation to vote on which they like best. Put this motto at the front of your church publications and/or on your letterhead, and look for ways your church can faithfully demonstrate its truth.

9. *Do the "Sabbath Swap."* Inform your congregation that next week they should come to church in the same clothes they usually wear on Wednesdays at work, home, or school. If they wear "church clothes" to work, they can carry a briefcase or bring something with them that represents their everyday life. Instruct them to think, talk, and act as much as possible the way they do on weekdays, and have them likewise do the "church thing" on Wednesday. During your midweek service, or for a short time in the following week's worship service, break into groups of four to six and talk about the differences between people and circumstances and the difficulties they encountered in trying to be the same on a weekday as they are on the Lord's Day. Encourage everyone to consciously work at making their behavior and attitudes pleasing to God at all times.

6

I Like Church, But It Should Serve This Broken World

The Spirit of the Lord is on Me,
because He has anointed Me
to preach good news to the poor.
He has sent Me to proclaim freedom
for the prisoners and recovery of sight
for the blind, to release the oppressed,
to proclaim the year of the Lord's favor.
—*Jesus*, Luke 4:18-19

"Do you know who lives in that house?" my mother inquired as we passed a 50-year-old wood-frame bungalow in Jackson, Michigan. Although Jackson had been my home through high school, it had been more than 20 years since I moved away. How could she expect me to know who lived in what house? With little curiosity, I answered a quiet "No."

Undeterred, Mom continued, "Maybe I never told you that story. Barbara, who lives in that house, came into the office a few years

ago. After her time with the doctor she
stopped at the receptionist window where I
was stationed. As I arranged her billing account and next appointment, Barbara volunteered, 'My husband left me, I'm all
alone, I'm sick and poor, and nobody cares.' I
looked up at her and said, 'Why, Barbara, I
know someone who cares. May I come see you
tonight?' "

My mother knew what it was to be poor
and lonely. In the Great Depression, while
she was in high school, her family had been
evicted when the bank foreclosed on their
house. Despondent, her mother committed
suicide. Without faith in Christ at that
time, it was a season of poverty, rejection,
and bitterness. So Mom could identify with
brokenness.

That evening she visited Barbara. My
mother listened to her woes, wept with her,
and comforted her. Then she opened a Bible
to show Barbara how much Jesus loved her.
Faith awakened in Barbara's heart—she became a Christian believer. She also became a
part of Mom's small group Sunday school
class.

Barbara was one of the walking wounded
of this world. Broken and traumatized souls
are found in every nation, city, and zip code.
Christ's church bears a responsibility to sustain the hopes and dreams of this broken
world. You will love your church when it joins
Jesus in serving these hurting people. In

fact, in your heart of hearts you no doubt long
for this servant attitude to characterize every
congregation.

Jesus specialized in helping and healing
the wounded. "...The people brought to Jesus
all who had various kinds of sickness, and
laying His hands on each one, He healed
them" (Lk. 4:40). He took time to visit with
people, physically reaching out to them, even
the lepers whom none dared touch.

When Jesus cared for broken humanity, it
wasn't with the indifferent attitude of the
state bureau of motor vehicles or the unemployment office. He passionately preached
good news to those who were overwhelmed
by all the bad news. He brought liberation to
people bound by sin and demons. Jesus made
Himself available, touching hands and eyes
with healing, feeding the hungry, defending
the accused, and associating with the dis-
reputable. Humility marked everything Jesus accomplished for the poor and needy; He
remembered that His human roots began
with the poor in a stable.

Jesus had the wonderful ability to look at
a sea of faces and see individuals needing His
love. He could also look at one wounded soul
and see the pain of the world in that person.

We live in an era of unparalleled commu-
nications that supply a steady stream of information about our broken world. In recent
years I've followed Pol Pot's killing fields of
Cambodia, Idi Amin's wars in and around

Uganda, the Hutus and Tutsis bloodbath of Rwanda, and the genocide of townsfolk in the former Yugoslavia. I've tracked famines in Ethiopia and 70 percent unemployment in Haiti. In World War I, 90 percent of the casualties were soldiers. In the Bosnian/Croatian/Serbian war, 90 percent of the casualties have been civilians, including too many innocent boys and girls. Our world is a terrifying place that produces rivers of blood. And our ability to see, to hear, to feel, and to respond is being shut down, desensitized, with this inundation of evil.

The brokenness is not only overseas; it is all around us. Pornography invades the Internet, while television mocks morality and marriage. In many places, a high school pregnancy is no longer a shame but a badge of honor, something to boast about. Marriage is devalued through living together without vows and defiled through "no fault" dissolution. We are ashamed of politics and suspicious in business.

What do we do about it? Escapism is in vogue. Housing developments are built with gates to protect dwellers from those we don't know, trust, or like. Sometimes we're not all that excited about the pastor challenging us to reach out to the poor and the powerless. But our churches should do more than act for self-preservation, like gated communities filled with people who look like us, act like us, believe like us, and don't rock our boat. The desire to worship and fellowship in comfort and without tension is easy to understand. It just doesn't correspond to our Lord's command to go into all the world with the gospel, alert to the needs of the poor and broken.

Old instincts lead some to think they want a church that avoids the harder issues of a struggling world. But residing deeply in the heart of each newborn believer is the longing to be like Jesus, to serve His mission in power, and to know that He is pleased with their church.

Jesus Loves the Poor of This World

Jesus was anointed or commissioned by God's Spirit for a special ministry to the poor (see Lk. 4:18-19). He was called to care for the needy, and He expects us to share that calling. He instructed, "But when you give a banquet, invite the poor...and you will be blessed. Although they cannot repay you..." (Lk. 14:13-14). The first church at Jerusalem asked Paul to "remember the poor, the very thing," he said, "I was eager to do" (Gal. 2:10).

Many categories of specialized church ministries are prevalent today. Positions that quickly come to mind include Youth Pastor, Director of Christian Education, Minister of Music, and Administrative Pastor. If Jesus were to serve on a church staff, I suspect He would request the title of Pastor to the Poor.

Jesus does serve on church staffs, or at least He expects to. As He prepared His disciples for Calvary and His departure from this

world, He emphasized that He would be in
them to continue and to complete His ministry. "If anyone loves Me, he will obey My
teaching. My Father will love him, and We
will come to him and make Our home with
him" (Jn. 14:23). "I am the vine; you are the
branches. If a man remains in Me and I in
him, he will bear much fruit; apart from Me
you can do nothing" (Jn. 15:5). Jesus continues His work among the poor through
churches and Christians in whom He lives.

How Can You Serve the Poor?

Remember Barbara, the lady left desti-
tute by her husband, who felt nobody cared
for her? She not only lacked money, she also
lacked a sense of personal value. Barbara
learned to see worth in herself as my mother
cared for her on multiple levels. She discov-
ered she had a Savior, a new friend who
would be there for her, and a small group
who would include her. My mother and her
small group provided not only words, but material help as need required. Most of Barbara's life affirmation for years ahead came
through these sources. A broken person was
restored to near wholeness because one
woman offered her time and resources. You
can serve the poor by keeping your eyes and
ears open. Watch for God to bring someone in
your life for you to help.

Mom's church became one that regularly
reached out to the broken with gentle hands
of love. Whether my mother and her class

were influenced by the church or the church was influenced by the class I cannot confidently say. But I believe that a few can set the pace for the whole. And I know that one person can be used mightily by God.

How Can Your Church Serve the Poor?

On a larger scale is the story of Pastor Tommy Barnett and the First Assembly of God of Phoenix, Arizona. Tommy moved from Davenport, Iowa, in 1980 to pastor a church of 250 people. Today that church has 14,000 in Sunday worship attendance. *Moody Monthly* has honored Phoenix First Assembly repeatedly in the last ten years as one of the fastest growing churches in North America.

How did this come to pass? Pastor Barnett's answer is, "We try to find a hurt, and when we do we kind of jump up and click our heels. Because we found out that when we find a hurt and heal it, we've got the attention of God."[1] Others often ask Tommy, "How can I get God's presence within my church?" Tommy's answer comes from his personal Bible study. He observed that the little lady who dropped her small coin in the offering plate got God's attention. The sparrow that falls from the tree limb, the homeless beggar who reaches for food, and the suckling baby who cries out get God's attention. It dawned on Tommy, "If I could just

---

1. Tommy Barnett, "Enlarge Your Circle of Love," plenary session message, Evangelistic Association of New England, January, 1996.

round up all the people that nobody else wants and bring them to church, I'll have the attention of God."[2]

Over the years, many ministries have been started at First Assembly. They've bought buses to bring in children from other neighborhoods. They've welcomed a score of ethnic and language groupings. Included in the circle of love are prostitutes, bikers, street people, and gangs. The church maintains 193 weekly ministries to the broken. Jesus is pleased.

What we need to remember is that Tommy's church didn't begin with nearly 200 ministries of compassion. Fifteen years ago they were a modest-sized church with one or two ministries. Smaller churches that can't do everything can do something, and that something is the place to start. The average church in North America has 102 constituent adults—102 adults who are not present every Sunday. Ministry to the poor and broken is not the responsibility of a few score megachurches. There are more than 400,000 North American churches whose participation Jesus expects.

Churches of all sizes are engaged in caring for prisoners and their families through Prison Fellowship. For many years my church youth group ministered weekly to the juveniles of the county youth detention center. Sunday mornings began at eight o'clock

---

2.   Barnett, "Enlarge Your Circle."

with a church service for incarcerated kids.
Sixteen- and 17-year-old Christian teenagers
established friendships, brightened the
holidays, and showed Jesus' love to the im-
prisoned young people. It wasn't a large,
complicated program; it was just a simple
outreach to heal a broken world. You may not
feel comfortable starting with a prison program. Just start somewhere.

Jesus Loves the Disenfranchised of This World

"He took a little child and had him stand
among them. Taking him in His arms, He
said to them, 'Whoever welcomes one of these
little children in My name welcomes Me...' "
(Mk. 9:36-37). Jesus identified Himself with
every child to the extent that He said we
serve Him when we help or encourage children. He followed up His affirmation of children with an emotional warning: "And if
anyone causes one of these little ones who believe in Me to sin, it would be better for him
to be thrown into the sea with a large mill-
stone tied around his neck" (Mk. 9:42). Better
to die at the hands of the Mafia than to
wound a child.

A Chicago couple has been charged with
1,200 counts of child abuse against their four
children. The indictments include sexual
abuse, narcotic injections by needle, and use
of force to feed the children rats and roaches.
Patrick Murphy, a lawyer for the Cook
County Defenders Office, remembers that

ten years ago the county handled a child
abuse case once a month, and everyone in the
office would read the report with horror. Now
these cases come up 20 times a week, and no
one in the office is moved to review them except by assignment. In 1986 Cook County
had 8,000 children in custody. A decade later,
in 1996, there are 45,000 boys and girls in
government care, 45,000 children with "man-
gled psyches and emotions," according to Mr.
Murphy. The state of Illinois counts these
children at risk and plans for tomorrow's
prison needs accordingly. If the church
doesn't do something to help the children,
who will?

Churches and Christian individuals need
to act in behalf of children and orphans. God
sees Himself as "a father to the fatherless"
who "sets the lonely in families" (Ps. 68:5-6).
As His representatives in this world, church
people must do the same.

One Church One Child is a 15-year-old
organization dedicated to the adoption of
African-American children. Its goal is to re-
cruit at least one family from every African-
American church in the nation to adopt a
child. Seventy percent of the adoptable children in the land are African American, and
since 1986 One Church One Child has helped
60,000 of them find permanent homes. More
than patching a rip in the social fabric, the
group is restoring young lives through Christian homes and loving, praying parents. Jesus is pleased.

After a conference presenting the 50-Day Spiritual Adventure to Phoenix, Arizona, pastors and church leaders, I was standing in the parking lot of Orangewood Church of the Nazarene. My eyes rested on an attractive building next to the church. "Is that your administrative building?" I inquired.

"No," Pastor Marion McKellips replied. "That's our school for pregnant junior high girls."

"Did you say junior high girls?" I wondered if I'd heard what I thought I'd heard.

I had. A Christian lady within the church who worked in the public school system had a heart for junior high girls who were dropping out of school to carry their babies to term. Now the church provides the building and teacher while the public school supplies the teacher's salary. Young lives are salvaged instead of savaged. Years from now, scores of mothers will remember the love and care of a Christian teacher and a church that helped them continue their education. The Kingdom of God will grow.

Twenty years from now, who will remember that your church served a broken world? What would it take for you to help the children in your neighborhood, in this nation, in the world? If you don't want to duplicate efforts, look for ministries already in place in your town with which to link hands and efforts.

God's tender heart reaches out to the poor, the children and orphans, and the disadvantaged and disenfranchised, including widows. Jesus warned, "Watch out for the teachers of the law.... They devour widows' houses..." (Mk. 12:38,40). The early church ministered to widows (see Acts 6:1). It compiled a list of widows who were too old to work or remarry (see 1 Tim. 5:9). In case any church might be reluctant to assume this responsibility, James wrote, "Religion that God our Father accepts as pure and faultless is this: to look after orphans and widows..." (Jas. 1:27).

In northern Indiana is a church in which all the widows and widowers receive a phone call every morning. The elderly who live alone naturally fear falling or having an illness, because no one would know or come to assist them. The Helping Hand Outreach, as they call it, goes beyond this originating church to reach other area churches and in some cases unchurched elderly people. Every morning the phone chain begins, and if at any home no one responds, a personal visit is made.

While many are talking about the homeless, churches and families in the Boston area are bringing street people right into their own living rooms. Responding to a 1984 call to provide shelter for a homeless family, Faith Church of the Nazarene of Hingham, Massachusetts, began regularly providing

short-term housing for needy families.
Dorothy Newell, who founded the Friends of
the Homeless with her husband Rev. J. Scott
Newell, remembers their first family, a couple with two children. The father had just
lost his job at the Quincy shipyard, which
closed that same year. Since then the New-
ells have sheltered hundreds of homeless
people, most of them from the south shore
area of Boston. They've made this possible
through the participation of many churches
and host Christian families. What makes
Christians willing to share the privacy of
their homes and belongings? They have compassion for distressed people with a basic
need. Without shelter, couples with young
children can end up living in abandoned
buildings, automobiles, and cardboard boxes.

We all should be moved with compassion,
remembering the church's founding apostles
who suffered want themselves. "To this very
hour we go hungry and thirsty, we are in
rags, we are brutally treated, we are homeless," Paul described (1 Cor. 4:11). Our Savior's heart is moved by the homeless, for He
identified with them: "Foxes have holes and
birds of the air have nests, but the Son of
Man has no place to lay His head" (Mt. 8:20).

Reach Out and Touch the World

After escaping bombs and fires in Sudan,
living in an overcrowded refugee camp in
Kenya, and traveling across the world, the
Kara family is adjusting well to their Min-
neapolis home. The Karas are a few of the

millions of disenfranchised people around
the globe who have endured refugee camps
and sailed the oceans in boat flotillas while
fleeing war, hate, and starvation. Through
churches and church families, World Relief of
Wheaton, Illinois, has resettled 115,000 refu-
gees. Rose Kara and her five children, ages 2
to 16, came to the Twin Cities through the
Salem Covenant Church's sponsorship.

Rose's husband, a surgeon in a small
clinic, was killed when northern Sudan in-
vaded the south, killing the Christians. Rose
and her children walked the entire way to
Kenya. Eighty thousand people made this
trek, many not surviving due to exhaustion.
The Salem Covenant Church took God's challenge to the Israelites as its own: "And you
are to love those who are aliens, for you yourselves were aliens in Egypt" (Deut. 10:19).
Church member Harley Schrech, far from
feeling this aid was a burden, said, "It has
been a gift. We have learned so much...."[3]

There are many ways to touch the broken
world. Youth mission trips have great value.
Such trips may be costly, especially in view of
how little can really be accomplished in a
week or ten days. But the greater work is
usually a lifetime transformation in the
teens themselves. The mission trip is not an

---

3. "Sudanese family adjusting to life in the Twin
   Cities," *St. Anthony Bulletin*, February 15,
   1995.

end in itself, but a seed of compassion and mercy sown for a lifetime in malleable hearts.

Lifestyle Serving

We must serve this broken world—and keep on serving. God calls us not to an event, but to a lifestyle. My parents learned that with Barbara.

Thanksgiving Eve has long been glorious and beautiful for the Luptons. It was customary for the church I pastored to gather together for a meeting of praise and testimony. Afterward we would move into the fellowship center to complete the evening with laughter, goodwill, and Thanksgiving pies.

One Thanksgiving the church surprised Nancy and me with a generous food shower. This was a totally unexpected act of love from the congregation. I'd planned to drive my family 200 miles to my parents' home that evening. Since the trip could only begin after church festivities were over, we would arrive in Jackson, Michigan, around 2:00 a.m., which would still allow us some sleep before a warm Thanksgiving family gathering. As Nancy and I packed the food shower away, I suggested we take a few sacks to my parents. We had eaten off their table for years during our frequent visits, and Dad and Mom wouldn't take money from us. But how could they refuse a gift of groceries?

My parents had the good sense to not wait up for us—we would visit all Thanksgiving

Day. Upon our arrival, Nancy and I quietly brought in several boxes of food. It was so much fun that it felt like we were playing Santa Claus to parents—a role reversal! Nancy opened the cupboard to begin putting the groceries where they belonged. With a startled gasp she called for me to look. The cupboard was barer than Mother Hubbard's. There were no cereals, no canned goods, no spices, no bags of sugar or flour. I opened the refrigerator, and while it was clean and shiny, it had no food either.

We had come upon a mystery. My parents were expecting us for Thanksgiving dinner, but instead of the sights and smells of holiday food everywhere, there was no food in the house. Nancy and I had the bewildered joy of restocking the shelves and refrigerator. Thanksgiving morning my parents were as surprised at the refilled cupboards as we had been at the empty ones the night before.

The mystery was not so mysterious to those who have learned to serve the broken and needy. My mother had learned that Barbara—yes, the same lady introduced at the beginning of this chapter—was out of food and money. Mom suggested to Dad, "I think the Lord wants us to give our food, including our Thanksgiving meal, to Barbara." Dad quickly agreed and they loaded the car. Dad and Mom had so much joy in giving away the food that they didn't stop until it was all gone.

As we visited, Mother noticed the two loaves of banana nut bread Nancy had placed on the counter, and she began to weep. She said they freely gave all the food away except for one loaf of banana nut bread, which she had made for Thanksgiving Day. Mom argued with the Lord that Barbara would receive all the other food, and that she didn't need the loaf of bread too. But God's nudgings moved her to give all—to include the homemade holiday loaf. What joy to wake up the next morning and find the cupboards refilled and the banana nut loaf replaced with two from her daughter-in-law!

"Cast your bread upon the waters, for after many days you will find it again" (Eccles. 11:1). Scripture is often given to understatement— Mom and Dad weren't required to wait many days. Even as they were emptying their shelves to provide for a poor divorcée, the Lord was leading Nancy and me to fill our car with food to restock those empty shelves.

Compassion and mercy have never been spectator sports. There is a tension between prayer and duty. We must pray for this broken world, for everything ultimately depends on God. But our prayers must also lift us from the sidelines to the battlefield, for God will often work His life-changing wonders through us individual Christians and our churches. We are people under Jesus' kingship who invade the kingdoms of this world. We invade not to conquer, but to serve, and as we serve, we conquer nations, cultures, and hearts.

In the history of the world there have been
no more than
one hundred thousand really great
men and women.
And of that number, eighty thousand or more
came from humble, poor homes.

❖ ❖ ❖

The measure of a person's greatness
is not the number of servants employed,
but the number of people he or she serves.

❖ ❖ ❖

...I tell you the truth,
whatever you did for one of the least of these
brothers of Mine, you did for Me.
                    —*Jesus*, Matthew 25:40

Make It Happen

*These suggestions will get you started
in serving a broken world.*

Individuals

1. *Go on a "vision quest."* Search for ways you can serve the world right around you. Ask God to show you people who need your help, to open your eyes and mind to new ideas and opportunities to serve. Once you've settled on an area of need you can be actively involved in—whether it be homelessness, distressed children, illiteracy, lonely seniors, or something else—start looking for specific ways you can carry out your mission to the broken.

2. *Go on record.* Sometimes we find it easier to put off doing something because we've kept our plans to ourselves. When we vocalize plans to a friend who'll be likely to ask about them later, we become more motivated to carry them out. Talk about your desire to write to a prisoner, to visit a nursing home, to open an after-school Bible club. Then set a date to begin your service venture, and let that be known. The people you talk to will take an interest in your plans and will encourage you to keep on serving.

3. *Get involved in the news.* The bad news you see on TV or read in the newspapers becomes overwhelming because you just can't solve all the world's problems. But you can do *something.* Start with just one story.

Inspect the news for people who are hurting, and design a way to reach out to them. Perhaps you can make a specified mission donation for a country that's going through a famine or war. You might take a lifeguard course and volunteer a weekend each month at a beach on which a tragic drowning occured. Or simply send a sympathy card or fruit basket to a mourning family you've read about in the obituary column. Set a goal for yourself to do a little something whenever a news story catches your attention. Your active interest will contribute to the healing of the world's brokenness.

Families

4. *Take a trip to the hospital.* Set aside a family night to make up care packages for a local pediatrics ward, nursing home, or veteran's hospital. Call for suggestions from the nurses on what their patients might enjoy: used magazines or comic strips, homemade cookies, toys or puzzles, personal hygiene items, or crafts to keep them busy. Then set a special appointment time with the staff—or appear during visiting hours—to deliver your care packages as a family. Be cheerful, interested in patients' problems, helpful in any way you can. If you have performers in the family, put together a poetry reading, skit, or selection of songs to keep patients entertained, to get their minds off the pain they're feeling. By coming in contact with those in

need, your family will more easily sympathize with others.

5. *Adopt a missionary family.* Check with your church mission committee or call a local or national mission to find a family that's similar in ages and interests to yours. Take a night to write personal letters to each family member, to learn their names and study a little bit about the country in which they serve. Encourage your kids to write their new friends to find out what they'd like for Christmas or birthdays, then help them purchase and send the items they choose. If at all possible, obtain a photo of the family. Paste the picture on a "missionary jar" to which your kids can contribute any loose change or a tithe from weekly allowances. Include your kids when you write a check to the overseas family, or when you receive their monthly newsletter or financial reports. If you'd like to adopt a native missionary (who's from the country he or she is serving), contact Gospel for Asia mission at 1-800-WIN-ASIA (946-2742).

6. *Instigate a monthly family service night.* Set aside the first Tuesday, last Thursday, or second Saturday—whatever fits into your schedule—to serve the broken world. You may agree on a certain service project you'd like to do every month, or you may want to devise a different project for each family service time. Mark those days on a calendar and plan ahead so you're sure to be committed. Serving a meal at a homeless

shelter, baby-sitting for an unwed mother, cleaning up trash on a city street or stretch of highway, reading to children at a local library, or helping with seasonal decorating at a retirement home are all activities that will bolster your relationship as a family as well as serve those in need. Be creative, and make this family service time something you all look forward to. After you're through serving, go out for ice cream or just spend some time together discussing what happened, how God used you, and what people said that showed their appreciation for your involvement.

Churches

7. *Find your place on the map.* Set up a bulletin board featuring a map of the world above a small table holding push-pins, tags, and a pen or two. Ask individuals and/or families to pin their names to a country and pledge to pray for that region of the world. Use the bulletin board to post news articles about countries or people-groups who are in immediate need—those suffering from natural disasters, wars, relocation, etc. If your denomination provides mission project opportunities, or if your church has connections with other organizations that go overseas, you may want to place that information on the board as well. Keep your congregation informed of ways they can help with prayer and physical and financial support.

8. *Plan a community-cleanup service.* Instead of a regular church service, spend your

after church fellowship time or your Sunday school class or youth time picking up litter and doing any general maintenance you can at a local park, forest preserve, parking lot, or highway section. Be sure to provide baby-sitting so parents don't have to look after younger children. Explain to participants that by taking care of the earth and cleaning up the community, you are showing God's love for His creation and His people. Sing praises while you clean; don't be shy about talking to people who ask what you're doing; let your service to God's world be an act of worship.

9. *Highlight community and/or national service organizations.* Invite World Relief, Opportunity International, World Vision, Compassion International, your denominational mission, or any other Christian services—as well as Habitat for Humanity and other helping-oriented organizations—to set up displays in your narthex or fellowship hall. During the worship service, advise your people to spend some time finding out about these groups and how they might participate in serving the world with them. If you have the time and freedom within the structure of your service, ask the spokesperson for each group to give a short testimony. Your church may even consider giving money or time to one or several of the outreaches.

7

I Like Church, But Where's God?

Father, I want those you have given Me to be
with Me where I am, and to see My glory...
                              —*Jesus*, John 17:24

As a teenager I liked church so much that
if the building was locked, I would break in.

This was a large, high-profile church, but
back then the building wasn't well secured.
The youth group met an hour prior to the
evening service, and some of us would show
up early—before the doors were opened. One
out-of-the-way entrance was fastened with a
hook and eye. Opening it was a "no brainer."
I would take the church bulletin, slip it between the door and jam, and slide it up until
it knocked the hook out of the eye. When the
custodian came later to open up, he would
smile knowingly. We were already inside.

In church I found nearly everything I
needed. That probably sounds nerdy, but it
was true, and it was exciting. I made my best
friends at church. Life there was a constant

celebration. The wisdom of the church helped me understand all my circumstances. I established lifelong worship habits in its sanctuary.

I also encountered God—and that was the main thing. I felt I met God in worship. I often heard Him speak to me in the messages. I saw His Spirit work at the altar. There was no doubt about it. God came to my church.

I'm writing this chapter on Palm Sunday afternoon, shortly after returning home from church. This isn't the church of my youth; it's not even in the same state. But I met God in the service again this morning. As we drove home, my wife said, "I think that was the best worship service I've been in at this church." Hyperbole is acceptable when you're lauding others. We had spent an hour and a half praising the Lord, and now Nancy was praising the praise. I knew what she meant. She too had experienced God.

All my life I've been going to church and meeting God. I need Him more today than ever. I would feel cheated if I went to church and didn't feel the touch of the supernatural. As a teenager I had so many needs, and they were wonderfully met through church programs and people. Today, my needs are more simple: I need God. I need to hear from Him. I need Him to accept my worship. I need to talk to Him. I need to know that He is in charge of life's bewilderments. I long for God, especially when life is confusing.

King David understood this. "As the deer pants for streams of water, so my soul pants for You, O God," he wrote. "My soul thirsts for God, for the living God" (Ps. 42:1,2a). David needed to know that God was there and watching over his life. He was in a high-stress situation. Rare is the person who doesn't search for God when her child is in the hospital or when he is going through a personal crisis.

He continued in Psalm 42:2b, "When can I go and meet with God?" Why would he ask a question like that? He had met God during many insomniac nights (see Ps. 63:6). He knew he didn't have to *go* to any special place to meet the Lord. God was everywhere. David said it himself: You can't hide from God, even if you try (see Ps. 139). All he needed to do was pray, and God would be listening.

But the king was longing for a kind of divine encounter that was different from private prayer and personal Bible study. He wrote Psalm 42 at a time when the nation was at war and he was away from Jerusalem. He reminisces about "leading the procession to the house of God, with shouts of joy and thanksgiving among the festive throng" (Ps. 42:4b). In today's vernacular we would say he longed to encounter God at church.

That probably sounds like a hunger you have as well. Sure, you go to church to see friends, to teach or sing, and for any number of commendable reasons. But if you didn't meet God there, you wouldn't keep it up—not for long. If God's presence isn't obvious at church, before long the main incentive for attending is gone.

What kind of worship experiences do we look for at church? Some want traditional worship with hymns and forms from the past. Others prefer a contemporary-style service with worship choruses and a sense of spontaneity. Why do we prefer one style over another? Most of us prefer a worship format that helps us, even frees us, to get in touch with God. My worship preference includes music that reminds me of earlier good times with God, that lifts my heart with joy and praise, or moves me to confession and prayer. That's true for most of us. Just as some men feel dressed for work in a suit and tie, while others are dressed for the same kind of work in a polo shirt, so some of us are prepared to meet God in traditional worship where others are ready to meet God in another style. For all of us, however, the question is not one of style, but of encountering God.

God Expects to Meet Us at Church

Jesus promised to never leave us or forsake us—to always be with us (see Heb. 13:5). You can meet with Him at your work station, on a hike in the mountains, or traveling overseas. But Jesus also guaranteed, "where two or three come together in My name, there am I with them" (Mt. 18:20). Whether we're scattered during the week or gathered on the Lord's Day, God wants to meet with us.

Both individual and corporate meetings have long been important. God met with

Moses personally at the burning bush, and He met with the entire congregation as "the cloud covered the Tent of Meeting, and the glory of the Lord filled the tabernacle" (Ex. 40:34).

The tension between meeting God individually and meeting with him congregationally needs to be appreciated, not resolved. The battery under the hood of my car has two poles. If I use one pole without the other, the car won't start. But when I properly connect both poles to the engine, I have all the power I need. Does God want to meet with me in my personal quiet times? Yes! Does He want to meet with me along with the rest of the church? Yes again! Your spiritual power is at its greatest when you connect with God both on your own and through His family.

The church was off to a great start shortly after Jesus' resurrection. Three thousand people were converted the first time Peter spoke in public, and thousands more came to Christ the second day. But this didn't mean things were easy. The same leaders who crucified Jesus arrested Peter and John. Soon the blood of martyrs would begin to flow. Should the believers scatter to their own homes and keep silent prayer vigils? That might have sufficed; the Lord would still have heard. But instead, "they raised their voices together in prayer to God," and at that church meeting they found the One they were looking for: "After they prayed, the place where they were meeting was shaken. And they were all filled with the Holy Spirit and spoke the word of God boldly" (see Acts 4:23-31).

I read about a horse-pull in Canada. One horse pulled 9,000 pounds. A second horse pulled 8,000 pounds. Teamed together they pulled not 17,000 pounds, but 30,000 pounds. Similarly, God's power through the church is greater than the sum of His power in our individual lives. God meets with you and with me. But when He meets with *us*—the church—His power is at its greatest.

God Wants to Meet All of Us Every Week

Encountering God isn't just for big people and Bible scholars. It's also for little people and all subjects of the King.

The disciples were annoyed when parents brought their children to Jesus to have Him touch them. If I had been a parent who witnessed the power of Jesus' hand, I'd have wanted Him to touch my kids too. But the disciples rebuked those parents: "Don't you have any sense? These times together are designed for adults. Children have short attention spans. They wiggle and giggle." Jesus, however, was indignant with the Twelve. "Let the little children come to Me," he said. "Do not hinder them" (Mk. 10:14).

Matt 21:15

The Palm Sunday parade was more pleasing to Jesus. That's when children were shouting in the temple, "Hosanna to the Son of David!" This time the disciples didn't complain—they'd learned their lesson! But the chief priests said, "Do you hear what these children are saying?"

"Yes," Jesus replied, "have you never read, 'From the lips of children and infants You have ordained praise'?" (Mt. 21:15-16).

Jesus touched me in my childhood times at church, just as He touched the children long ago with His blessing. My earliest memories are of the action songs and the "flannel graph" pictures. My teachers told the Bible stories with love and passion. The Lord stirred my heart in those formative years. I also remember being in the prayer meeting each week. One time as we sang, a man next to me took the hymnbook from my hands, turned it around, and gave it back to me. I was too young to know I was holding it upside down! Listening to the testimonies and the impassioned prayers made the greatest impression of all my early encounters with God. He was in those meetings, and I knew it.

Church isn't for corralling and controlling children while the parents are being renewed. Church times are for Jesus to bless *everyone*. The First Christian Church in Traverse City, Michigan, plans its worship services to include children. Kids light candles to open the service. Youngsters hear a well-prepared talk or object lesson that complements the whole of the service. Older children serve as ushers and musicians. This congregation is burgeoning—its worship services are filled—because the whole family encounters God together.

The Protocol for Meeting the King

If church is for children and all subjects of the King, then it should be of value to review the correct way to meet our King. *Protocol*—do you remember the word? I saw an interview of an actress who practiced her curtsy for hours. She was training herself in the protocol for meeting the Queen of England. In a court of law, for an offense as minor as a traffic ticket, the bailiff demands that all rise for the entrance of the judge and that everyone in court remain respectfully silent. The judge must be addressed as "Your Honor." That is the protocol. Paul wrote, "...I am writing you these instructions so...you will know how people ought to conduct themselves in God's household, which is the church of the living God...." (1 Tim. 3:14-15). At church we are in the presence of the King and Judge of the universe. Let's practice proper protocol when meeting with Him.

Protocol Begins With Getting Ready

"Come near to God and He will come near to you. Wash your hands, you sinners, and purify your hearts..." (Jas. 4:8). God invites us to come to worship Him, but He wants us to be prepared. To meet a monarch, you would wash up, style your hair, polish your shoes, and dress appropriately. Meeting a king or queen or president doesn't begin when you are received into his or her presence. It starts days before, with anticipation and preparation.

When I was growing up, like most of my school friends I had two pairs of shoes. One was my everyday pair; I wore those to school, at play, and for most of life's "regular" moments. The second pair was called "church shoes." These were worn to weddings, funerals, graduations, or any other extremely important occasion, including church services. When my everyday shoes wore out, my church shoes became my everyday shoes, and a new pair of church shoes was bought. (My folks hoped I wouldn't outgrow both pairs at the same time!) Saturday nights were set aside for getting ready for church. I polished my church shoes, took my bath, did my Sunday school lesson, and got ready to meet God.

For me the two went together. Polishing my shoes was part of my heart preparation. God said to "wash your hands...and purify your hearts" to get ready to meet Him. For me that meant, "Polish your shoes, take your bath, study your Sunday school lesson, and say your prayers—tomorrow is church!"

When people complain that they don't meet God in church services, I sometimes wonder, "Were you up till midnight the night before? Did you get out of bed late in the morning, dress yourself in five minutes, and rush to church without cleaning your heart? No wonder you didn't sense that you met God! He was there for others, but you weren't ready for Him." The truth is, the more time we spend preparing to meet the Lord, the more likely we'll be to encounter Him.

Protocol Includes Humility

Part of the reason we "fuss" over getting ready to meet God is because we recognize how much bigger He is than we are. He is pleased when we have that perspective.

The Bible explains God's relationship with His people in terms we can appreciate. For instance, the Bible says, "God opposes the proud but gives grace to the humble" (Jas. 4:6b). We understand that, because we do the same thing. I heard a cowboy say, "I try to be nice to everyone, but I don't take much guff from anyone." That's a loose paraphrase of what God says. You've undoubtedly encountered an arrogant, pushy, "people user," and you find yourself resisting and avoiding that person. But then you come upon someone with a cheerful, humble, serving spirit, and you welcome every connection with him or her. We all oppose the proud and prefer the company of the humble.

If you want to meet God when you go to church, prepare yourself, and then enter His house with humility. God declares, "I live in a high and holy place, but also with him who is contrite and lowly in spirit" (Is. 57:15b). Humility does not barge into the presence of the King, but enters meekly with a bow and a kiss of the hand.

The New Testament Greek word for worship is *proskuneo*, which means "a reverential kiss." "Kiss the Son," wrote the psalmist (Ps. 2:12). That sounds odd to Western minds, but what it means is that we should meet Jesus with reverent submission and humble affection. He longs for your kiss. Remember Jesus' dinner experience in the home of Simon the Pharisee? I imagine the table was set with beautiful flowers, the finest linen, and the choicest foods. But instead of praising Simon, Jesus sadly commented, "...I came into your house...[and] you did not give Me a kiss..." (Lk. 7:44-45). Simon was so busy thinking about his own importance as a religious leader that he forgot about the significance of his guest. A humble kiss of greeting might have given his heart a better perspective.

Humility also teaches that God is important enough for us to be at church on time. Plan to arrive 15 minutes early, then if for some reason you're five minutes late, you'll still be there ten minutes ahead of time! You wouldn't arrive late for a visit with the state governor. If you're consistently late when you meet with the Lord, what does that reveal as to how important He is in your mind?

Go to church in an attitude of expectancy, believing that God will be present, ~~anxious to~~ eager make Himself known to those who have come looking for Him. How unfortunate, for whatever reason, to go to God's house and have it be nothing more than human encounters. Letting that go on year after year would be even worse.

Protocol Involves Praise

The recognition of God's greatness naturally spills over into praise. So when we go to church, we humbly "enter His gates with thanksgiving and His courts with praise" (Ps. 100:4a).

People were created with an impulse to praise. Whenever I see a rainbow I point it out to Nancy. If she sees it first, I hear about it from her. We are compelled to *ooh* and *aah* over these delights. The Book of James teaches us that every good thing in life comes from God (see Jas. 1:17). That means we should count the daily *oohs* and *aahs* of the Lord's goodness to us. Then we bring these to church. As our great King, God deserves our constant praise. What a joy it must be to Him to hear a whole congregation praising Him together.

Praise puts out a welcome mat, proclaiming, "God, we love You and we welcome You here." As the psalmist wrote, praise creates a home on earth for the Lord: "But Thou art holy, O Thou that inhabitest the praises of Israel" (Ps. 22:3, KJV). When God hears praise, I believe He feels like He has come home.

The last decade has witnessed a praise renewal in church gatherings. Many congregations engage in not just a song or two, but extended times of singing their compliments to God. Believers in these churches readily admit to meaningful encounters with God while praising Him.

To meet God in church, start getting ready early. You might even want to listen to Christian radio or a worship tape so that you're preparing and praising at the same time. Then, remembering how wonderful God is, enter the sanctuary and find your seat. Bow your head and take some time to humbly say to the Lord, "You are my God, and I've come to worship You. I offer my kiss of reverence." Let this humble act and the corporate praise of your church body lead you to a worshipful meeting with God.

God's Surprises

It is possible to be with the Lord and not be all that aware of His presence. All too often people leave a service with no sense of having encountered God. Their car bumper sticker would read, "I like church, but where's God?" Don't despair; that's been happening since the church's beginning.

Two of Jesus' followers trudged down a long, sad road on that first Easter morning. Their leader was dead and buried, and life seemed dismal. Then Jesus came along and joined them in their walk, but they had no idea who He was.

If Jesus had turned away after an hour, they might never have known they had walked with the risen Son of God. When Jesus stayed and taught them from the Scriptures, their downcast ears still didn't recognize His voice. It was only when the Lord broke bread with thanksgiving that "their eyes were opened and they recognized

Him" (Lk. 24:31a). Jesus had been there for hours, but it took them a while to become aware of Him.

Jesus is in our church services whether we are aware of Him or not. We all have times when we need Him to break through our dullness with an unexpected encounter.

A pastor friend greeted me at a conference recently, and I inquired how his church was doing. He beamed. "Great! God is doing wonderful things in our church," he replied.

For me, that wasn't an answer but a teaser. "I'm glad to hear that—tell me about these great things God is doing."

It seems the Spirit had nudged him to preach through the Epistle of James, and he soon began to sense God was at work. As he preached week by week, there was a stirring among the people.

Two weeks before our conversation the text had been, "Submit yourselves, then, to God. Resist the devil.... Come near to God and He will come near to you. Wash your hands, you sinners, and purify your hearts, you double-minded" (Jas. 4:7-8). As this pastor neared the end of the sermon, he knew God was speaking to hearts. He improvised the close of the service. In a step of faith, he asked those who felt moved to commit themselves to a renewed life of holiness to come to the front of the sanctuary for a time of prayer. Half of this large congregation approached the altar in tears; the other half remained in their seats with their own tears. After that meeting, each congregation member was assigned to a support or accountability group. God had met with them as a church, so they felt a solitary walk would not sustain them.

God came upon them in an unusual encounter that morning. Five hundred lives were touched in a way that would never have happened if each person were worshiping separately.

When You Need Him Most

Maybe you're longing for such an experience, a time when God is so obvious to you that your emotions are affected. Maybe you're hurting, and you need Him to be there to comfort you as no one else can. To a people in exile, great pain, and confusion, God promised, "Then you will call upon Me and come and pray to Me, and I will listen to you. You will seek Me and find Me when you seek Me with all your heart" (Jer. 29:12-13).

Sometimes you feel so much pain that you don't want to go to church. Go anyway. Go and seek the Lord, and find Him in your need.

I was agitated and angry one recent Sunday morning. I knew this was not the best way to meet God. But I went to church anyway because I knew I needed to displace my anger with praise, because I hoped that somehow church would be helpful, and because I'm a church-going kind of Christian.

My anger was directed at someone important to me who had betrayed me, someone I

had loved yet now wanted to reject—with
God's blessing, of course. Nancy and I sang
the worship songs, and I found them surpris-
ingly moving. A dramatized Scripture presentation and testimonies all led up to a
message on the Good Samaritan who came to
the aid of a robbed and beaten traveler. Jesus
told this story to answer the question, "Who
is my neighbor?" He was giving an example
of how loving others shows we love God with
heart, soul, strength, and mind.

My pastor concluded the sermon with his
own question: "Who is *your* neighbor, the one
God wants you to love, the neighbor no one
else will touch with Christ's love if you
don't?" My heart was smitten and healed almost at the same moment.

In the car on the way home I told Nancy,
"The Lord spoke to me again this morning."
Tears began to run down my face, and I had
no words to continue.

Nancy quietly answered, "Yes, I know. He
spoke to me, too." We'd had another encounter with God.

I meet God in my private prayers, in my
praise over seeing a rainbow, in my morning
rising and evening going to bed. But some of
my greatest encounters with the Almighty
have been at church, with joyous music,
anointed preaching, the table of the Lord,
and the touch of the Spirit on my heart. I met
God in church as a five-year-old, as a teen, as
a hurting adult, and I expect to meet Him
again in church this week.

You can expect the same thing. When you need Him most, keep your heart open. You will find that God comes to meet you, for He too is looking for a rich encounter.

Through the week we go down into the valleys of
care and shadow.
Our Sabbaths should be hills of light and joy in
God's presence;
and so as time rolls by we go from mountain top to
mountain top,
till at last we catch the glory of the gate,
and enter in to go no more out forever.
—*Henry Ward Beecher*

❖ ❖ ❖

Speak, Lord, in the stillness,
While I wait on thee,
Hushed my heart to listen
In expectancy.

Speak, O Blessed Master,
In this quiet hour;
Let me see thy face, Lord,
Feel thy touch of power.
—*E. May Grimes*

❖ ❖ ❖

My Lord Sabbath
Welcome to my home.
Welcome to my heart.
Welcome to my mind.
Welcome to my spirit.
May this Sabbath/Sunday
Be filled with your Presence.
Amen.
—*Karen Burton Mains*

Make It Happen

*These suggestions will make it easier
for you to encounter God at church.*

Individuals

1. *Start Sabbath today.* Don't wait for the end of the week to sing praises to God. Find the music of your favorite hymn or chorus on cassette or CD at a Christian bookstore. Ask your pastor if you can borrow a church hymnal to help you prepare for the upcoming worship time, then read through a hymn every morning. (If you read a familiar one you'll sing it in your head throughout the day.) Sing songs out loud. Sing them with a friend. Play them on the piano, the guitar, or your stereo. Sing in the shower! Praising God throughout the week will get your heart ready to meet Him at church.

2. *Don't touch the sleep button.* Set your alarm clock so you can get to church 15 minutes early—before the service begins. Don't spend that extra time in the sanctuary talking with friends; spend it with the Lord. Spend time quieting your mind and preparing your heart by praying or by simply sitting in silence before God. Enjoy the musical prelude. Read through the hymns and/or choruses you'll be singing. Really concentrate on getting yourself ready to encounter God during the service.

3. *Check your "openness meter."* Are you concentrating on *viewing* what's happening

in church, rather than on *participating* in worship? Are you open to the possibility of God touching you in a way you never expected? Be careful not to put God in a box. Recognize that He is willing and able to surprise you! During the service, watch out for some common detractors: thinking about tomorrow's workday, criticizing the music and sermon, critiquing people's clothes or the way they treat their children. That doesn't mean you have to squeeze your mind into what is being said from the podium. But make sure any time your attention does wander, it goes to God and to what He might want to say to you.

Families

4. *Introduce the "To and Through" Game.* The rules are simple. When you go to church on Sunday, search for ways God might speak *to* you, then find ways He might speak to someone else *through* you. Family members of all ages can play this—and it's a good activity for the ride home from church or for after-church lunch discussion. You might report to your kids, "I was feeling kind of flustered this morning," (they may add, "We noticed"), "and God talked to me through the first Scripture reading, which said that His peace transcends all understanding and guards my heart and mind." Your five-year-old could tell the family, "Susie said her grandma was sick, and God talked through me when I told her I would pray that she'd get better." Don't be

discouraged if your to-and-through discoveries are slow in coming. With a little practice the whole family will get better at hearing God speak.

5. *Pay God compliments.* Worship involves attributing worth to God, and one of the ways we can best prepare to meet Him is by remembering His wonderful qualities. So spend time as a family—at the breakfast table, during Saturday evening quiet time, or before going to bed—telling God how great He is. Go around a circle and complete this sentence: "God, I like You because... (...You never sleep...You love me no matter what... You're always with me)." After every family member has voiced his or her praise, pray together, asking God to show even more of Himself to each of you.

6. *Plan a family praise night.* You can do this on your own, or invite another family or two to join you. Include younger people by asking them to teach you a praise chorus they've learned at a retreat or at camp. Older people in turn can share with them a hymn your church rarely sings anymore. If you'd like a step-by-step guide through an evening of praise, order the "We Will Glorify" video featuring the worship music of Twila Paris (call 1-800-2Chapel). It also includes tips on planning an "Agape Feast" for earlier in the evening and "tape turn off" suggestions so you can incorporate family discussion time.

Churches

7. *Be still and know.* Sometimes we spend so much time in church talking *about* God and *to* Him that we never get a chance hear *from* Him. If we have a relationship with God, that means the communication should go both ways! If your church service doesn't already include times of silence, suggest that your congregation spend a minute or so to be still before the Lord. David the psalmist, who seems to have encountered God in a way many Christians wish they could today, wrote, "But I have stilled and quieted my soul" (Ps. 131:2a). Provide a little time for your people to do the same.

8. *Hold a "worship only" service.* Although God can certainly speak through the ministry of the Word, He often uses music and prayer to reach beyond reason and touch us more deeply. Yet often church services center on the intellectual rather than the emotional. From time to time, allow God to touch people in a different way by changing the format of your service—announcements, sermon, and other talk can come next week (or print them in the bulletin). Work with hymns, choruses, and choir numbers, special piano solos or orchestrated pieces, and let people sing, pray, and listen to what God has to say to them. Invite people to come pray at the altar. Serve Communion, perhaps, even though it may not be the "usual day." And pray hard as you're planning the service. Let

God speak to you about the encounter with His people He desires.

9. *Disclose those close encounters.* Send a feature to your local newspaper or radio station about the "close encounters of the spiritual kind," that you've experienced at your church. Ask people in the congregation to contribute examples of times they really saw or felt God working in the service, and use those as quotes or sound bites. Then have someone—maybe a budding writer you'd like to empower—compile the contributions into a single article. Make it fun, playing off the idea that people from your church have had personal encounters with Someone from "out of this world."

8

I Like Church.
I Hope It Anticipates
a Great Future

*...I will build My church,
and the gates of Hades will not overcome it.
—Jesus, Matthew 16:18*

Watching an America's Cup race on TV, I
was awed as two of the world's finest sailing
vessels raced downwind in majestic beauty.
When they rounded the buoy marker for the
first return leg, the two boats were less than
three seconds apart. They zigzag tacked their
way upwind, and one pulled 20 seconds ahead.
Observers had never seen so much time gained
in one leg of a race. On shore afterward, the
two captains related what happened.

One captain exuberantly shouted, "The
winds were perfect today, the boat performed
well, and my crew was on top of everything.
We always knew which sail to set to catch the
wind. I hope tomorrow's weather is just like

today's." The other captain whined, "This was the worst race of my life. The sea was abominable; the wind was awful. We had no idea what we were doing. I hope tomorrow's wind is dramatically improved."

Isn't that the way life is? Some church leaders report, "What a wonderful time to be in the Lord's work. Satan is certainly active, but God's grace abounds. We are making friends in the community and ministering to needs. Several have recently become Christians; discipleship classes are seeing fruit. The Spirit of God, like a wind, is touching many lives." Others complain, "What a dismal time to be in the Lord's work. Immorality and unbelief are society's norm. No one seems interested in spiritual matters. I feel utterly bewildered for our church. I hear it was much easier to witness for Christ in the 1950's. Why was I born too late for the good times? Is there no hope and future for the church?"

Two boats under the same wind. One captain made the best of it and one made excuses. Thousands of churches across the land. Some are catching the wind of the Spirit. Others haven't learned to put up a sail.

What hope is there for the church—your church, my church, Christ's church? Have you heard despairing statements like, "I like church, but it seems to be less important in our culture;" "I liked church as a kid—it's probably still good for kids;" or "I like church, but it's not really relevant these days"? Did the church only span the era from first-century chariot races to black-and-white television? Has its day now come and gone?

This is not just a sociological question. It is a matter of passion for many of us. Investors buy stocks hoping for a prosperous future with the Dow Jones average. The college graduate joins a new firm hoping the company is strong, that he hasn't attached himself to a dying organization. As a Christian, I have the same aspirations for the church. I long for the church to have a bright future. I rejoice in its strengths, grieve at its weaknesses, and would love to know its best days are just ahead.

Some signs indicate that the church is declining; some reveal that the church is on the ascent. When autumn arrives a tree drops its leaves. In spring the leaves grow back. The tree's prospects are not in these seasonal changes, but in the health and strength hidden from view within its trunk and under the soil. Likewise, the prospects for the church aren't in cultural trends or the opinions of its cynics. The future of the church is in Christ and His resurrection. Easter secures the church's future for now and eternity.

Easter and the Church's Warranty

The end of their days together was near—the cross loomed ahead. Jesus was ready to pass the baton to His disciples. But did they

understand His mission? Had they rightly
recognized Him? When He was gone from
this earth, would they carry on His plan and
work for His Kingdom? It was time for a long-
range strategic planning retreat in which the
disciples would look at the core issues and
Jesus would ask the hard questions.

The retreat spot was carefully chosen.
The city, Caesarea Philippi, was 100 miles
north of Jerusalem and only 50 miles from
Damascus. This was the farthest from Jerusalem Jesus ever ventured with His disciples. The ancient city, a global crossroads,
had some unique religious characteristics.

The holy retreat would be held in the
shadow of pagan gods. William Barclay cited
14 temples of ancient Syrian Baal worship in
the immediate area.[1] Caesarea Philippi was
also the site of a great hill containing a deep
cavern. A spring in that cavern was the leg-
endary birthplace of Pan, the Greek god of
fertility and nature. The legends of Greek
gods flourished in Caesarea Philippi. The
Hebrew patriarchs were also acquainted
with this region, and the influence of the
Jews was present within the city's Jewish
synagogue. But there was more. At Caesarea
Philippi stood a great temple of white marble
erected to Caesar. No one could approach the

---

1. William Barclay, *The Gospel of Matthew*, Vol. 2,
   (Philadelphia, PA: Westminster Press, 1975),
   134.

city without seeing that glistening white marble temple and thinking of the might and declared divinity of Rome.

This is true drama. Jesus, a homeless, penniless carpenter from Nazareth, gathers 12 rather ordinary men around Him. The Orthodox Jews are plotting to destroy Him as a dangerous heretic. Jesus stands surrounded by the temples of the Syrian gods, in the haven of the Greek gods, next to a gleaming temple to the Roman gods, in the heart of Hebrew history, and He asks the disciples who they believe He is. They answer, "The Christ, the Son of the living God" (Mt. 16:16). With all the gods of the world listening, Jesus is proclaimed the Anointed One, the Son of the one true living God. The disciples were declaring, "The gods of these temples are not alive. But there is one living God, and You are His Son."

In response, Jesus says in essence, "Some of these temples are already near ruin. The practice of religion rises and falls. But I will build My church, and it will not fail. The temples around us are not the way to Heaven; they are more like the gates of hell, keeping its people in bondage to fear and death. These gates shall not prevail against the prayers and evangelism of the church. My church will grow, will endure all storms, and will end victorious. The temples here are built of stone, and men have keys to open them. My church will be built on the sturdiest rock, and you shall hold keys to the very Kingdom of Heaven."

Jesus didn't say He would build His temple, which might have meant white marble. He didn't say He would build His synagogue, which would have been limited to a Jewish context. He said He would build His church— *ekklesia*, "an assembly of people called out of the world."

"I will build My church." Jesus would handle the building process. He would ensure its rise. He would guarantee that the hellish powers couldn't beat it down. The church's prospects were as bright as the prospects of Christ Himself. If death had defeated Jesus, then the church would have no guarantee.

Last year a friend bought a computer with a three-year store warranty. Six months later the store declared bankruptcy. Now if my friend's computer breaks, he's out of luck. The store warranty only lasts as long as the store. The security of the church, however, is as good as the life of Jesus Christ. His resurrection ensures the church's future.

Yet the resurrection of Christ is not all there is to the future of the church. Jesus gave the keys of the Kingdom to His followers. A key is an indication of ownership. My friends and neighbors do not have keys to my house; they come in only when I unlock the door and welcome them. Peter and the apostles opened the door of faith to the Jews at Pentecost (see Acts 2), to the Samaritans (see Acts 8:14ff.), and to the Gentiles (see Acts

10). Christ will build His church, but He gives us the keys and wants us to accept an ownership role, to open the door to the Kingdom for others.

When you go to a shopping mall, you are a consumer, not an owner. You don't hold keys to the stores; you just stop in when they're open, pick up what you need, and leave. What about your church? Is it your home, to which you hold a key? Or do you treat your church like a "store" that benefits you when you need it but doesn't require you to take an owner's responsibility?

Just as you have a physical key to your house, so you are one of the keys to the future of your church. Family members who hold keys to my home have roles to fill. I handle all the physical maintenance, the kids keep their rooms clean, and we all share in upkeep duties. Your church will have a brighter future when you, along with the rest of your congregation members, say, "This is my church. I hold one of the keys to its future. Where shall I serve?" The future of the church is dependent upon Christ's Easter warranty and your responsible key holding.

North Sharon, Michigan, is not visible on many maps. It's scarcely a place at all. The "don't blink at the stoplight or you'll miss it" jokes don't work with North Sharon because it's too small for even a caution light. The most outstanding thing in town is the North Sharon Church—a true country church.

The first time I was a missionary guest speaker there, I met fewer than 30 old-time members and a part-time lay preacher—and that was everybody. I thought "Thank You, Lord, for not calling me here to serve—this church has no future. It's time to close the doors and throw away the keys." Five years later I drove by the place and was stunned to find a large church building holding a congregation of 600 and a thriving Christian school. Six hundred members? I didn't think there were 600 people within a six-mile radius of the church!

The mystery is not all that complicated. A pastor came who believed that Christ wanted to build His church and that 30 key-holding members would unlock enough doors to make it happen. The pastor claimed the Easter guarantee, and each member claimed a key.

The Church's Easter Revival

Some authors have written with little hope when it comes to the church. A few years ago I refused to read many of the Christian magazines and newsletters that came to my home because I knew the news would be bad and the articles would moan, "Ain't it awful about religion and morals and education and government?" It seemed the editors hadn't heard about Christ's resurrection.

I also knew that "ain't it awful" writing was not a new trend. In the late 1600's and early 1700's much of the Christian writing was known as Jeremiad literature because of its woeful Jeremiah-like tone. The church of the American Puritans was in rapid decline. "It seemed to be a time of extraordinary dullness in religion; licentiousness for some years greatly prevailed among the youth of the town; there were many of them very much addicted to night walking and frequenting the tavern, and lewd practices...indeed family government did too much fail."[2] A hopeless sense of "ain't it awful" pervaded Christian leaders' views of their towns and churches.

Through faithful fasting, "concerts" of prayer, and powerful preaching, the Spirit of God brought about the first Great Awakening. Whole cities turned out to hear preachers like George Whitefield and Gilbert Tennent. "There were remarkable tokens of God's presence in almost every house. It was a time of joy in families on account of salvation's being brought unto them; parents rejoicing over their children as new born, and husbands over their wives, and wives over their husbands. The goings of God were then seen in his sanctuary...the congregation was alive in God's service, every one earnestly intent on the public worship."[3] This revival renewed the church and rescued nations on

2.   Jonathan Edwards, *Jonathan Edwards on Revival*, (Carlisle, PA: Banner of Truth Trust, 1987), 9.
3.   Edwards, *Jonathan Edwards on Revival*, 14.

several continents, beginning with England and spreading to many other countries.

A generation was saved, and church prospects brightened for 50 years. But like the cycles in the Book of Judges, there was a downturn late in the century. "It soon became fashionable to adopt views which avowed a disbelief in the Bible, scoffed at the divinity of Christ, and looked upon religions as a superstition of the past. Especially was this true of scholars...The colleges of the land became infected with the deadly contagion of unbelief...Lawlessness seemed to be the order of day. Religion was disregarded and morals were low. In many towns of considerable size, no places of worship were to be found...."[4] The infidelity of the French Revolution infected the world, and in many towns worship was said to be a tenth of what it had been.

During the first Great Awakening, evangelists held the hero status of Michael Jordan and Garth Brooks combined. By the 1790's that acclaim was given to the authors of atheism. "Infidelity in its most coarse and brutal form sneered at religion and scoffed at morality. The predominant sentiment of the people seemed to be: 'We will not have God to reign over us.' "[5]

---

4.   Frank G. Beardsley, *A History of American Revivals*, (New York: American Tract Society, 1912), 78ff.

5.   Beardsley, *A History of American Revivals*, 81.

College President Dr. Timothy Dwight pleaded with God to revive Yale University. He debated religion with Yale students. In the Kentucky frontier, pastors James McGready and Barton Stone prayed fervently. At last revival came to Yale University and to Kentucky like the Resurrection morning dawned on Jesus' discouraged disciples. In the East all the major universities were touched to the extent that religious infidelity was driven from campuses for 50 years. In the West Rev. George Baxter, who visited Kentucky, left this testimony: "On my way, I was informed by settlers on the road that the character of Kentucky was entirely changed, and that they were as remarkable for sobriety as they had formerly been for dissoluteness and immorality....A religious awe seemed to pervade the country."[6] The results of that second awakening were the overthrow of atheism, the spiritual renewal of the churches, and the inauguration of great missionary and philanthropic enterprises. A season of Easter—revived life—had come again to the church.

The cycle repeated again 50 years later as the United States approached the Civil War. A combination of heady financial prosperity from the gold rush and railroad expansion, and the ridicule of certain religious zealots

---

6. Beardsley, *A History of American Revivals*, 96.

whose prophecies about the return of Christ did not come to pass, resulted in a serious downturn for churches. Preaching seemed to have no effect—and scarcely an audience. Into this morass Christians entered with a mighty prayer movement remembered as the Layman's Prayer Revival. At the peak of the revival, one out of every four men in Chicago was in a daily prayer meeting. In Boston a traveler reported, "I am from Omaha, in Nebraska. On my journey East I have found a continuous prayer meeting all the way."[7] A million adults were converted in 12 months between the autumns of 1857 and 1858. Christians learned to pray and work together, laypersons took ownership in God's Kingdom, churches grew dramatically, and a social conscience against slavery grew firm. This revival circled the globe, covering Southern Africa, the South Seas, India, England, Ireland, Scotland, Wales, and other parts of Europe.[8] Later, the famous Welsh revival of 1904 powerfully impacted North America and the mission fields of the world in addition to the British Isles.

In 1932 a little group of businessmen in Charlotte, North Carolina, became greatly concerned about the spiritual and moral decay of their city. Twenty-nine persons came

---

7.   Beardsley, *A History of American Revivals*, 227.
8.   J. Edwin Orr, *The Fervent Prayer*, (Chicago, IL: Moody Press, 1974), xiiff.

together for a day of prayer and fasting. The time was such a blessing that they repeated this meeting monthly in different homes, including the farm of W.F. Graham, a dairyman who shared the hope for revival. In particular Graham was concerned about one of his own children, a teenage boy who needed to come to grips with God.

In 1934 this prayer team invited Mordecai Ham to come to Charlotte for a preaching crusade. It was there that young Billy Graham was converted. The team prayed for Charlotte and reaped the world. In 1949 Billy Graham preached a crusade in Los Angeles, sparking a seven-year revival that swept the United States and much of the globe. In the late 1940's, 49 percent of Americans said they were actively involved in Christian worship. By 1956 the figure was 62.5 percent. That decade captured an additional 13.5 percent of the population for Jesus. By the late 50's more than two-thirds of the children of America were receiving weekly Christian instruction.

We have fallen from the spiritual heights of 1956. Today the U.S. is in the valley that precedes either revival or judgment. God is again calling His people to fast and pray for spiritual awakening. Bill Bright has hosted powerful conferences on prayer and fasting. I've heard estimates that as many as one million people fast weekly or monthly for revival. Foretastes of revival have reached

many college campuses and cities. Our
prayers must join those of King David, who
was frightened for the spiritual condition of
his children, his grandchildren, and the nation of Israel, "Restore us again, O God our
Savior.... Will You not revive us again, that
Your people may rejoice in You?" (Ps. 85:4,6).

Spiritual awakening is like Easter to the
church. It brings new life to the dead. The future of the church is as bright as your readiness to post a memo on your bedroom mirror
reminding you to pray every day for another
Holy Spirit visitation. The future is as bright
as your readiness to join a vast multitude in
fasting and prayer for revival. The best day
for the church may be tomorrow. Pray that
your church and all churches will see another
great season of spiritual life and harvest. For
whenever the church has dislodged itself
from a prideful throne and cast itself upon its
knees, God has answered with a revival.

David Bryant of Concerts of Prayer International coined the phrase "streams of revival." When spring warmth melts the
mountain snow, the flowing water forms
countless rivulets, which come together to
build little streams, which join as the sources
of major rivers. Although we are not in a
spiritual awakening phase in North America,
many rivulets of revival are apparent. These
need to be recognized and nurtured:

- The U.S. National Day of Prayer has
  grown from an insignificant nicety to a
  day of spiritual power.

- The Denominational Prayer Leaders Network, incorporating scores of denominational leaders, meets annually to facilitate revival.

- Movements of prayer and revival, such as "See You at the Pole," are increasingly prominent in public high schools.

- In 1995, more than 20 college campuses experienced powerful sessions of confession and renewal.

- Citywide prayer movements are maturing in a variety of formats, including pastors' prayer summits facilitated by the Northwest Prayer Renewal.

- Thousands of churches are using the 50-Day Spiritual Adventure, which has nurtured the revival of numerous congregations.

- Citywide evangelistic breakthroughs have taken place. In Modesto, California, for instance, 30,000 people accepted Christ because of a two-month gospel drama presentation.

- Coalitions for moral righteousness are advancing in many regions.

- Promise Keepers has become a major tool of revival among men.

- Many churches continually experience dramatic renewal in praise and worship.

- Christians working in the secular society are becoming more vocal about their faith. For example, Ricky Skaggs and nineteen country-western musicians produced a video in which they give their Christian testimonies.

The earliest gleams of an Easter daybreak are dawning on the church, and with them comes the abiding hope for a great future.

Easter and Christ's Return

Jesus has promised to return with resurrection life. We anticipate the day when the angels shall proclaim, "The kingdom of the world has become the kingdom of our Lord and of His Christ, and He will reign for ever and ever" (Rev. 11:15b). The church looks forward to the bright prospects of reigning with Christ. "...If we died with Him, we will also live with Him; if we endure, we will also reign with Him..." (2 Tim. 2:11-12).

Perhaps the main biblical emphasis on the coming resurrection is to promote holiness and godliness in life here and now. "But we know that when He appears, we shall be like Him, for we shall see Him as He is. Everyone who has this hope in Him purifies himself, just as He is pure" (1 Jn. 3:2-3).

A century ago Blondin, the world's greatest tightrope walker, amazed his audiences with his stunts as he walked across Niagara Falls. Largely unknown is the fact that he placed a great star at the end of the rope and walked with his eyes fixed on the star. In the same way, the apostle John points us to the Bright and Morning Star and asks us to walk through the temptations of this life with our eyes fixed on Him. The prospects for the church today are brightest when God's people daily prepare themselves for the Lord's return by confession of sin and a longing to be holy.

Easter and Regeneration

The church's expectations are bright because the Spirit of God continues to bring Easter regeneration to individuals. When He raised Lazarus from the dead, Jesus offered a similar spiritual experience to all who were present: "I am the resurrection and the life. He who believes in Me will live, even though he dies; and whoever lives and believes in Me will never die..." (Jn. 11:25-26). The apostle Paul explained, "But because of His great love for us, God, who is rich in mercy, made us alive with Christ even when we were dead in transgressions..." (Eph. 2:4-5).

After Michelangelo had finished a sculpted masterpiece, the art critics came to judge his work. They marveled at the figure of the young man. One reportedly whispered, "You have indeed produced your masterpiece. It is perfect, lacking only one thing." With anxiety the great artist demanded to know the flaw. "You cannot correct it," the critic acknowledged. "Your work is humanly perfect; all it lacks is life." Even when we humans have fashioned our lives to the best of our skills, we still need the resurrection life of Christ.

New life in Christ. It's something we all long for. The same God who breathed life into a lump of fashioned clay and called him Adam is today breathing spiritual life into humble, repentant, believing hearts. The church in China is sustaining one to two million converts a month. A church within five miles of my home reported 2,000 professions of faith on one recent weekend. The future of the church is as certain as the next person who calls on Christ. The Spirit of God is at work in the land, and churches with a vision of their bright futures couldn't wish for anything better. They simply keep praying and pleading for one more soul to be birthed into the family of God.

"I like church. I sure hope it anticipates a great future." Rest easy. The church has marvelous days to look forward to. It has survived seasons of growth and seasons of pruning. It has experienced winters of difficulty and springs of revival. But the church is still here, despite all it's been through, and Christ is committed to its success.

But don't rest *too* easy. Christ is building His church—but He's using you and me to build it. What will you do to advance your church? What will you do to ensure that it has a great future? Will you take the responsibility of one who holds the Kingdom keys? Will you pray for the resurrection life of Christ to come to a friend, a coworker, or a relative? Will you commit yourself to participating in the Spirit-led movement toward personal prayer and fasting? Will you cleanse your life morally and spiritually in expectation of the Lord's return?

The future of the church is assured in the warranty of Jesus' promise to build it, in the hope of revival awakenings for the church, in the coming return of Christ, and in the very personal Easter-style regeneration of individual believers. Its prospects become even brighter as we family members put to use our keys of ownership, as we fast and pray and purify ourselves.

That is when the Spirit takes over. We aren't required to be the wind that propels the church through the uncharted waters of the future. We just need to stop complaining, put up the sail, catch the breeze of the Spirit, and experience the power of the Resurrection.

I love Thy kingdom Lord, the house of Thine abode,
The Church our blest Redeemer saved,
with His own precious blood.

For her my tears shall fall,
for her my prayers ascend;
To her my cares and toils be given,
'til toils and cares shall end.

Beyond my highest joy, I prize her heavenly ways,
Her sweet communion, solemn vows,
her hymns of love and praise.

Sure as Thy truth shall last, to Zion shall be given,
The brightest glories earth can yield,
and brighter bliss of heaven.

—Dr. Timothy Dwight

Make It Happen

*These suggestions will keep you
looking forward to the future*

Individuals

1. *Remember where you're headed.* Sometimes we get so wrapped up in the details of everyday life that we forget we're on a journey that will end in Heaven. So take some time to reflect on what it will be like to be physically with God. Recollect your journey so far—all the trials God has brought you through and the joys He's blessed you with—and then think about what is to come—a new earth, the peace and joy of knowing you are perfectly in God's will. Imagine coming into God's presence and meeting Him face to face instead of seeing "but a poor reflection as in a mirror" (1 Cor. 13:12) as you do now. Pull yourself away from the busyness of your schedule for just a few minutes to look forward to the future God has promised. Then praise Him for what He's planned for you.

2. *Enjoy the moment.* This isn't a contrast with remembering where you're headed; rather, it's another aspect of it. Take special notice of everything God has for you right now, and enter into it with your whole self. Instead of lamenting over the past and worrying about what will happen tomorrow, let yourself listen to the bird singing outside your office window, savor the meal that's been spread before you, sleep hard through

the night—because these are the pleasures, routines, or difficulties that God has given you for this moment. "Whatever you do, work at it with all your heart," Paul wrote (Col. 3:23a). So although you're looking forward to the end of the story, be sure to live fully and contentedly in each chapter.

3. *Rehearse an "eternity phrase."* Choose certain words to remind you that you and your church family are at the beginning of a wonderful time together. When you're discouraged or stressed out, repeat those words to yourself to help you put things into perspective. For example, remind yourself, "In a hundred years when I'm in Heaven, I won't even think about this," or "Isn't it great that this problem will soon pass away, and I'll be living somewhere perfect?" If you train yourself to see things from an eternal perspective—as God sees them—you'll soon find the little irritations and terrible inconveniences that once left you feeling hopeless are far from significant in your life.

Families

4. *Set spiritual goals.* Start a family tradition of evaluating your spiritual lives together. Each member of the family can report on how he or she is feeling about his or her spiritual journey, tell about encouraging indications of growth, and explain where he or she would like to improve. Your 12-year-old might want to add a few verses of Bible reading to each day; your teenager could hope to

invite more friends to youth group events; you may wish to add a regular half-hour prayer time to your week. Hold each other accountable by gently asking, "What have you been reading about lately?" or "I'd be happy to pick your friend up for church this week," or "Is there a way I can free up some of your time so you can pray?" Scripture Union's age-appropriate materials can help your whole family dig into the Bible and guide your personal prayer time. Why not order a copy (call 1-800-224-2735 to order) for each family member and check back together when you finish a study to reevaluate and prioritize your spiritual goals?

5. *Award Future and Hope certificates.* One simple, concrete way to encourage each other during tough times is by making a visible reminder of all that you have to look forward to. A certificate given out during family times together can be a fun vehicle for the message, "Even though you feel down and out, you're an up-and-coming superstar in God's plans!" Certificate forms are available in office supply shops—or let "border coloring" be a Saturday afternoon project for your upper elementary-aged kids. You can include in each certificate a relevant promise from God's Word: If Daddy is sick, write, "The Lord will sustain and restore you," or when your high school senior has fallen out with her friends, write, "The Lord will deliver you from times of trouble." Don't forget that everyone appreciates a lighter touch at times.

"There are no final exams in Heaven," or "When you live with Jesus your best true friend never moves away," or "Your riches in God's savings account will never be grabbed by earthly creditors" can really help to put life's hurts into perspective.

6. *Hold a "well done" dinner.* No, this isn't a burnt-meat-and-mushy-rice meal; it's a celebration of your spiritual victories. Use Jesus' words from Matthew 25:21 to verbally affirm each family member's spiritual progress. The head of the household should apply Jesus' words to each person's situation: "Well done, good and faithful servant! You have been faithful in talking to your friend Cathy about Jesus. He will put you in charge of many things. Come and share your master's happiness!" This is a great way to promote short-term spiritual growth and to let your family know that God is preparing them for bigger "assignments" in the future.

Churches

7. *Display hopeful signs of revival.* Tell about encouraging happenings in your weekly bulletin or on an overhead projector screen before your worship service. Include news of worldwide church events, prayer movements in your city or the nation, uplifting quotes from church leaders, statistics from evangelistic campaigns—whatever you can find to show that God is moving. Your local newspaper, other pastors, and ministry newsletters will have some great facts for

you to relate to your congregation. Or, call 1-800-224-2735 for information on signs of revival in North America. Your people need to know that the church in North America and around the world has great days ahead!

8. *Create a future-of-the-church banner.* In large letters, write "[YOUR CHURCH NAME] IS A CHURCH WITH A FUTURE" across a piece of butcher-block paper or oversized poster board. Ask everyone in your congregation to write a personal blessing on the banner. Imagine how exultant your pastor and leaders will feel each time they walk by so many well-wishes! Hang the banner in a prominent place so anyone who sees it remembers that God has great plans for your church.

9. *Celebrate church history night.* Highlight the key events of your congregation's background or of the church overall in an evening "Look How Far We've Come" service. This time can be silly or serious, simple or elaborate; but be sure to emphasize that God has brought you through the years because He wants to build you as His church. Do short skits about the starting of the youth group or men's prayer breakfast, present costumed monologues of special speakers or previous pastors who have had a considerable impact on your congregation, sing songs that have been meaningful to the church, or recite poems of promise and scriptural blessings. You may even want to divide into small

groups and brainstorm goals for the church and ways to achieve them. End with church-wide prayer, thanking God for all He's brought you through and requesting His direction in the great future He has planned for you.

10. *Participate in a 50-Day Spiritual Adventure.* Thousands of churches and hundreds of thousands of individuals have journeyed through **The Church You've Always Longed For** Spiritual Adventure that coordinates with this book. For information on how your church—and you as an individual—can participate in stirring spiritual revival with churches all across North America, call the Chapel Ministries at 1-800-224-2735 (1-800-461-4114 in Canada) and ask about the 50-Day Adventure.

Other
Destiny Image **titles**
you will enjoy reading

WHEN LIFE BECOMES A MAZE
by David Mains.

Life is full of mazes. Finances, jobs, relationships—all present labyrinths to our muddled minds! So what do you do when you get stuck in one of life's mazes? Here David Mains shares principles he learned while negotiating paths in his own mazes!

TPB-192p. ISBN 1-879050-77-3 (4" X 7")
Retail $6.00

Internet:
http://www.reapernet.com